Braving the Thin Places

Other Books by Julianne Stanz

Start with Jesus

Braving the Thin Places

Celtic Wisdom to Create a Space for Grace

JULIANNE STANZ

LOYOLAPRESS.
A JESUIT MINISTRY
Chicago

LOYOLA PRESS.
A JESUIT MINISTRY

www.loyolapress.com

Scripture quotations are from *New Revised Standard Version Bible: Catholic Edition*, copyright
© 1989, 1993 National Council of the Churches of Christ in the United States of America.
Used by permission. All rights reserved worldwide.

Cover art credit: javi.ruiz/iStock/Getty Images, M-image/iStockphoto/Getty Images, Miodrag
Kitanovic/iStockphoto/Getty Images, YuliaBuchatskaya/iStock/Getty Images

ISBN: 978-0-8294-4886-3
Library of Congress Control Number: 2021943000

Printed in the United States of America.
22 23 24 25 26 27 28 29 30 Versa 10 9 8 7 6 5 4 3 2

For Wayne, Ian, Ava, and Sean

Contents

At the Threshold of a Thin Place

*Irish seanfhocal (old word): An rud nach fiú é a
lorg, ní fiú í a fháil.
Translation: What is not worth seeking, is not
worth finding.*

Each of us stands at the threshold of a thin place, and we are its
gatekeeper.

Have you ever held a loved one's hand as they slipped from this life and
into the next? Birthed a child and felt the thin edges of God's presence
inside your being? Beheld such beauty that it took your breath away? Or
been moved to tears by an image or a piece of music? If so, you have stood
at the edge of a thin place, a place where God and humanity meet in a
mysterious way. These moments open us to places of rawness and beauty.
Something seems to break open inside us, and words are inadequate to
describe what we are experiencing. We feel a sense of breakthrough as we
break free of the ordinary and into the extraordinary.

We stand at the threshold of a thin place. We are gatekeepers to a
sacred chamber of the inner world. We can open the door and welcome others into this inner space, or we can close ourselves off to the
world around us. Sometimes we close the door so tightly on these
spaces in our lives that they have to be broken completely open to let
the light in.

Thin spaces are wild, messy places where God is at work.
Time seems to stand still, there is a discernible sense of sacredness, and the world around us speaks its own story to those who are listening. The concept of a thin place is an ancient one, arising from the Celtic tradition, but it holds real meaning for each of us today as we try to make sense of the world around us and, indeed, within us.

The Celts, known for their love of threshold places at the edge of life, such as Sceilg Mhichíl, a crag off the coast of County Kerry, were never afraid to explore God in the known or in the wild, barren edges of life. We should not be afraid either. The Celtic imagination considers sacred places to be "thin," or places where the veil between the worlds of heaven and earth seems especially permeable, and the worlds discernibly close to each other. Thin spaces exist between the now and the not-yet. Entering thin spaces is an opportunity that we don't normally have—to slow down, to pause, to look with fresh eyes, to recover a sense of wonder about the world. The pace of life moves too fast for many of us over concrete and inhospitable ground, and we are searching—for joy, forgiveness, healing, completion, and peace. God is all around if only we recognize his presence. And for those who do, that thin space is one of rejuvenation and renewal.

Thin spaces exist not only outside us but also within us. Each of us stands at the threshold of our own pain or wonder, our own thin space.
In each person's life are thin places where that person experiences God's presence in a way that stirs the soul. In these thin spaces we are broken open, and we encounter ourselves, our relationship with others and with God, in a deeper and more authentic way. Truth makes its home in these broken-open places, and we often receive the gift of new insights and memories. As we become more understanding,

compassionate, and authentic, we open up to new ways of seeing, fresh avenues of thinking, and ultimately, transformed ways of being.

Thin places are often associated with specific ancient or significant historical sites, such as Newgrange on the eastern coast of Ireland or Iona in Scotland. Growing up in Ireland, I frequented many thin places, and among my favorites are Glendalough in County Wicklow and Browneshill Dolmen in County Carlow. I have experienced the power of thin spaces—outside of myself and also within myself. A few years ago, I brought a group of pilgrims from the United States to Ireland, many for the first time, and witnessed the power of such thin spaces to affect people. Allison, who had no Irish heritage or background, upon arriving in Glendalough, suddenly knelt on the ground and wept. When I asked her why, she said, with tears rolling down her face, "I can't explain it, but I feel the presence of God here as I have never felt God before. I feel like a part of me belongs here. How can this be home to me although I have never been here before?" What she was experiencing was the edge of her own thin place.

The Heartbeat of God

Thin spaces are places in which you can feel the heartbeat of God.

The Celts did not live as if God were far away, and neither should we. God who was near and dear to the Celts is the same God who can be near to us. One of my favorite thin spaces is the first time that I held my newborn son, my first child. As I held him skin to skin, I felt his heartbeat against my own heartbeat, our hearts beating together. To this day, it stands out as a moment in which I felt closest to God. The Celts were inspired by looking to God at the heart of life, not away from life, much like the beloved disciple John, who leaned against Jesus at the Last Supper, listening to God's own heartbeat. We all have these moments too, just as the Celts did, times when our hearts beat in unison with God's own heart. This is the heart of Celtic spirituality—the spirituality of my ancestors, whose hearts still beat in unison with mine, whose lives are tied to the landscape of Ireland, to the rugged and sometimes-harsh hills and rolling rivers that are both beautiful and daunting. The souls of our ancestors who have passed are firmly present in a new way when we tap into the memory of our thin place.

Thin spaces bring to birth in us a greater yearning for God, and also a sense of belonging.

In thin spaces we get a glimpse of heaven, right here on earth. And, God knows, we need a little bit of heaven on earth these days!

The year 2020 was a defining one for many of us. A pandemic raced across the world, and phrases such as "social distancing" and "cocooning" became part and parcel of everyday conversation. Fear gave way to anger as civil unrest spread like wildfire throughout the world, and especially in the United States as voices called for an end to racial injustice, inequality, and disparity. The world seemed to be turning upside down the health of our economy, our people, our systems, and our structures. This upside-down world became a battleground on which to divide and conquer, and conversations about spiritual health were downplayed and set on the back burner. It became clear that underneath the anger and pain, the raw anguish of dispiritedness was and is still longing for a voice.

Beyond 2020, in a time of unrest, social upheaval, and intense communal pain, we push the boundaries of what is known for what is unknown. People express their pain in all kinds of ways: numbing it, cajoling it, wallowing in it, and acting out. We cry out for justice without knowing exactly what a just society looks like. We break free of and push against all kinds of barriers such as gender, race, and sex, and we find that walls that once seemed impenetrable are more permeable and porous than we expected.

All this reminds me of a line from *Les Misérables*, "Do you hear the people sing, singing the songs of angry men?" People are singing a song today, and we have to ask ourselves, Are we listening to that music? When we see widespread unrest, protest, and anger, what we are witnessing is the release of an interior tension; where what has been trapped inside is displaced as our own spiritedness, our voice, finds release.

Although none of us has the ability to predict the future, it's clear that this unrest will continue to manifest unless we address its root causes instead of just the symptoms. In the hectic pace of life, it is hard to find time to slow down and take time to reflect upon our lives. But it is necessary now more than ever.

While thin places have always been associated with specific ancient locations, I believe that we, as a collective humanity, in our yearnings and longings, have entered such a thin space today, a "thin time," a broken-open time, a time of spiritual displacement.

Thin spaces do displace us—from our comfort zones, from the way we think life should be—and they invite us to consider what to do with our pain and our longings. And if we step back and ask ourselves three questions, it becomes clear that we are living through a time of intense spiritual displacement:

- What are people doing with their pain today?
- How is that pain being expressed?
- How might we respond to their pain?

Henri Nouwen, the Netherlands-born theologian, in his 1982 book *Compassion*, writes, "One of the most tragic events of our time is that we know more than ever before about the pains and sufferings of the world and yet are less and less able to respond to them." If this rings true for you, and I suspect that it might, then you'll agree that we as a people must respond to the thin edges of people's joy, hunger, pain, desperation, and hope, especially when it comes to conversations about faith and spirituality.

So, how do we do this? For millennia, religion offered a path to understanding and a better life. But in the United States religion does not seem to offer the release, the comfort, and solace that it once did. More and more people are "voting with their feet" and leaving established religious traditions, frustrated with the "same old, same old" mentality that seems to typify mainstream American Christianity. We all want to be known and loved. We want authentic relationships and are all weary of in-your-face salesmanship and slick marketing. *And that goes for Christianity too.* Young adults in particular are tired of Christians who tend to focus on what I call their "glory stories" typified in narratives such as "I once was lost but today I am blessed to live this superabundant life exemplified by X, Y and Z." They often ask what happens in the in-between, for they instinctively know that it is in such a broken-open time that the real work of living happens. This is where the joys and struggles of life collide with the power of the Gospel message, where fear gives way to faith, despair to hope, and where redemption is possible, no matter the mistakes you have made.

This is a conversation that we all must break open today especially if we are to reach younger generations. Countless research has affirmed that young adults have little interest in formally joining a parish or signing up for a parish committee—and who can blame them when the vision of Christianity that is often peddled to young people is the Gospel of "nice"? Or the seemingly constant scandals that seem to plague Christianity that are incompatible with the Gospel? Such safe and antiseptic religion does not reach our wounds or help them heal. For people in pain today, the deepest questions of the heart are voiced in apathy, addiction, depression, anxiety, and despair, all of which researchers tell us are increasing, particularly in young adults.

If spirituality is a way for us to live out what we most value—our relationship with God and with others—then our hurts, longings, and brokenness can be made whole in the light of our faith. Today, however, the conversation has been moved or displaced from our churches onto the streets and onto the blogosphere without any reference to God or to the bonds that bring us together. In the court of public opinion, where trial by social media is quite real and dangerous, we see the danger of living out a disembodied spirituality: a way of thinking, acting, and living without a relationship to God who created us for him and for one another. This spiritual displacement finds its voice in communal expressions of pain such as protesting and social media trends, and in rioting and civil unrest. Lest we think that these are new ways of "acting out," remember that in the Scriptures we see people acting much the same way: tearing down false idols that had been turned into gods and calling for truth (transparent conversations), justice, and peace.

It is clear that we have entered an epoch marked by upheaval and spiritual displacement but also one characterized by a deeper search and longing for God. What's going on? I believe that we have as a people entered a thin space, a threshold place, an in-between place where fear and pain are palpable and pervasive. If we can navigate this well, we can emerge stronger, more connected to one another, more empathetic, peaceful, and hopeful—and as a result, we will be able to solve problems differently by working together. One way of navigating this thin space effectively, both within ourselves and as a society, is by drawing from the wellspring of ancient spiritual traditions, especially those from the world of the Celtic spirituality.

The Gifts of Celtic Spirituality

For more than twenty years I have spoken throughout the world on the topic of spirituality and integrated lessons from my Celtic roots into my talks, retreats, and writings. In packed conference halls filled with people from all walks of life and religious traditions, and in small rooms filled with Vatican officials, cardinals, and bishops, I have spoken of the power of faith and spirituality in a way that is as accessible and familiar as sharing a lovely cup of coffee or tea on a damp day. In sharing my story, I hope it becomes a bridge for others to find their own story and recognize their own thin spaces as places of prayer and renewal. Those who come to my retreats, talks, and seminars share their hopes and dreams but also their spiritual exhaustion and weariness with life, with their faith, and many times with God. This is expressed in their guilt for being a less-than-perfect Christian, wife, father, son, daughter, or friend, or in the shame of wounds that transport them to the past and from which they struggle to be free. Many of the elements of Celtic spirituality are big enough to wrap around us in these times, to comfort and restore us, to guide and nurture us.

Like an old quilt stitched together from familiar, comfortable fabric, the elements of Celtic spirituality emphasize the simplicity of a back-to-basics approach. A Celtic understanding of ourselves is familiar and yet unfamiliar at the same time. Celtic spirituality is the form of spirituality that developed in the ancient Christian churches of Ireland, Scotland, Brittany, Cornwall, Devon, Wales, Galicia, and the Isle of Man. Today, Celtic describes the languages and respective cultures of Ireland, Scotland, Northern Spain, Wales, Cornwall, the Isle of Man, and the French region of Brittany, but the term *Celtic* actually corresponds to the Celtic language family, which includes the still-spoken languages of Scottish, Irish, Galician, and Manx (Gaelic languages) as well as Welsh, Breton, and Cornish (Brythonic languages). The Celtic tradition as practiced today is one that builds bridges between the old and the new, the familiar and the unfamiliar, the known and unknown, between people and places, memory and imagination. It holds wisdom and newness for every person because the lessons and practices transcend time and culture.

Through the years I have introduced thousands of people to the richness at the heart of the ancient traditions I grew up with, for I was raised in an area of Ireland that is known as the "ancient East." This part of Ireland has deep rootedness in the Celtic tradition, and in speech, practices, and traditions it still retains many ancient elements that we can access today. The prayers and traditions of Celtic spirituality settled into my bones, carried me through many struggles, and strengthened the practice of my Catholic faith. Many other spiritual traditions such as Native American spirituality will find spiritual threads that are held in common with Celtic spirituality. This might make some uncomfortable, but *the lessons I draw from Celtic spirituality in this book in no way oppose any of the central tenets of Christianity and are compatible with the richness of Catholicism.*

Since Celtic spirituality has become popularized, it has lost much of its sacred depth and instead become cheapened and stripped of its relational roots. I am especially wary and weary of those who peddle Celtic spirituality as a cure-all or a secret arcane framework stripped of its essential DNA: the message of Jesus Christ, who came to save us all, and teachings about how to grow in friendship with God and the world around us. The elements of Celtic spirituality are not secrets; instead, they rest in the hands of those who keep them alive by passing sacred prayers and traditions from one generation to the next, guiding others to recognize the thin places in their lives as spaces in which God is felt and near.

Spirituality must be rooted in relationship: relationship with God and with one another. Those who strive to live the wisdom of the Celtic tradition find that it helps them become more attuned to God's presence. It teaches them how to navigate difficult times in life, thin times when we break open by the grace of God, or fall apart, run over by the pace of life.

At the heart of Celtic spirituality is the interplay among God, humanity, and the world; among light, twilight, and darkness. This interplay is often expressed in the Celtic love of thresholds, boundary spaces where time and emotion are marked differently than in the everyday. The edges of pain and pleasure, anger and joy, become blurred, and a thin space opens for those who have eyes to see it, ears to hear it, and hearts to feel it. Thin spaces have no sharp corners—they are not so blatantly defined. Rather, they are locations of nuance, not quite in time-space and not quite outside it. They are capable of cupping our pain and transforming it into something beautiful.

Throughout this book, I make references and share insights from this precious spiritual tradition that transcends time, space, and culture. I also share insights from other spiritual traditions, including Franciscan, Benedictine, and Dominican spirituality. You do not need to have any background in these traditions to draw from their strength and wisdom. Instead, we will journey together as pilgrims who dip into a sacred well and drink from all these practices that will strengthen, comfort, and restore us.

Searching for God is an act of abandonment, a wild adventure in which we leave the known for the unknown, the comfortable for the uncomfortable. In short, we break out of our comfort zone into a thin space. When we find the courage to do this inner work, we are broken open and become truly free. We change, our relationship with God deepens, and we find healing and wholeness in our relationships with others. We draw others through our light, our authenticity, and our vulnerability. We become tenderhearted and compassionate instead of hardened and bitter. We feel whole and wholesome and see ourselves, others, and life in a new way. So join me on this journey as we dip into this thin space where a great wellspring of spiritual wisdom awaits.

As the Irish wise word, or *seanfhocal*, says: "What is not worth seeking, is not worth finding." Seek and you shall find. Let's break open our thin spaces together.

Part One

Entering In

The world breaks everyone and afterward many are strong at the broken places.

—Ernest Hemingway, *A Farewell to Arms*

1

Who Are You?

*Always remember in your heart, these three
things: whence you come, who you are and what
shall become of you.*

—From the Kildare Poems, fourteenth century

"Who are you?" Sister Anne gently asked as her eyes met mine. I was seventeen years old and sitting in my religion teacher's office. "Who is Julianne?" she persisted.

With this question, a river of tears poured out as I began to tell Sister Anne all about my family, my grades, and my hopes and dreams for life after school. Even as I said the words, I could feel how hollow and wooden I sounded. I was going through a particularly difficult time, questioning who I was, my purpose in life, and where I was going. As I continued my ramblings, Sister Anne stopped me wisely: "Julianne, I know that you have many gifts, and I've no doubt that you will do great things with your life, but you have to look beyond what is happening around you and look at who you really are. Who you are is not what you do or what you will do, or the family that you are born into, although that is part of your story. Dig deeper, Julianne, and think about who you really are."

Like most people, I had never thought about this question in any depth. My answer was the truth that cut me to the bone. "I have no idea," I replied. She patted my hand in understanding.

I didn't know how to answer, but I had a beginning.

Who was I and what did I stand for? With this question, I began to enter a thin space and break it open. Across all ages, generations, and cultures, people have struggled with these same big questions: Who am I? What is my purpose? Is there more to life than what I see? These questions are at the heart of what it means to be a human being; they will continue to be asked in the future as they have been down through the mists of time. For example, researchers commonly place Pythia, the Oracle at Delphi, as living between 1400 BC and AD 381 in ancient Greece. The oracle, a wise woman chosen to give insights into the will of the gods, was asked all kinds of questions that delved into the deepest part of the human heart. On particular days of the month, the oracle spoke on behalf of the god Apollo. Her answers could be direct, conditional, or ambiguous, depending on the nature of the question. One of the maxims inscribed in the forecourt of the Temple of Delphi was the phrase "know thyself." Those who came to ask Apollo a question were often given the answer "know thyself" no matter the situation or question.

How are we to know ourselves? And is it possible to know ourselves fully? When we look in the mirror, we see our reflection, and yet we know that what we see is not the full picture. The mirror reveals our appearance but does not capture our thoughts, our feelings, or our soul. The way we live, how we act, and who we surround ourselves with are further glimpses of who we are, but the full perspective on what exactly makes us unique will always remain a bit of a mystery. Because the mystery of life that is unfolding in each day is largely unknown to us, who we are reveals itself to others and even to ourselves, gradually, one moment at a time, one day at a time. Like ferns that unfurl as they grow, each of us unfolds as a human being in the experiences that influence us, the relationships that shape us, and the choices that define us.

So as a starting point, let's begin with the most basic question: *Who am I?* How would you answer this question?

Many of us would begin with our name, which is the first attribute that identifies us. We then might move on to where we are from, what family we are a part of, and what we do for a living. We might even reference personality traits and gifts that we have been given. We might sketch out features of the town we grew up in, our place in the family, and a little bit of how we see the world. If you had asked me who I was at the age of seventeen, I might have responded something like this:

My name is Julianne Donlon. I grew up in a small, picturesque village called Hacketstown nestled into foothills of the Wicklow Mountains on the southeast coast of Ireland. The "sunny southeast" as it is often referred to although that is being quite generous considering how much it rains in Ireland! My family lives in the shadow of the mountain Luqnaquille or, to use the Irish term *Lognacoille*, meaning "hollow of the wood," or more properly, the ancient word *Lugnacoille* meaning the "woods of Lugh." Lugh was the Celtic god of the sun and a member of the mythical, supernatural race of gods called the Tuatha De Dannan who inhabited Ireland before Christianity. The town I grew up in is typical of many small towns in Ireland, a place where everyone knows everyone else and everyone is often related to one another through blood or marriage. This closeness makes for a tightly knit community with bonds that stretch back generations, but the downside is that "people would live in your pockets if you allowed them to," as my grandmother Hannah often reminded me.

My childhood was spent playing outside with my friends for most of the day until six o'clock, when a robust shout "Come in for your dinner!" from my mother or someone else's mother sent us running home. Neighbors popped in for a cup of tea and a pinch of sugar, and one of my abiding memories of growing up was the conversation and chatter at the heart of the family home, often around the kitchen table. During those years of growing up, it seemed that all the problems we might face could be solved over a cup of tea and a chat with a friend.

What this story doesn't tell you, of course, is who I am. Who I really am, deep down in the core of my being. When we think about the question "Who am I?" we often respond with a litany of information that tells others what we do, our gifts, how we spend our time, and some of the people who are important to us. Where I grew up, how I live, who I surround myself with—all are important pieces of the puzzle that make up the picture of who we are, but these pieces are only part of our story. They barely scratch the surface of what's really going on inside of us. Very often, the person we *really* are is someone we run from, protect, or hide from the world.

By the age of twenty-three I was living in America with people I didn't know, looking out at a landscape that was completely foreign to me. "How on earth did I end up here?" I asked myself as I lay in a strange bed with the unfamiliar smell of coffee in the air. For my entire life, I had woken up to the sound of the tea kettle whistling in the kitchen, with the scent of peat and coal heavy in the air from the many open fires in the homes around my village. My journey from Ireland to a small town in Wisconsin is a familiar emigrant's tale: I left home to pursue work and a dream to experience life beyond what was familiar to me, to see more than the mountains I grew up with and to grow in new ways. Beyond the physical journey I undertook, the spiritual journey I was on—and am still on—is common to us all, because each of us is on a road through life. It doesn't matter if we stay in one place all our lives or travel elsewhere; we can't run from who we are.

The "who are you?" conversation with Sister Anne has stayed with me, even these many years later. For many years, I could not answer this question authentically. Only as I lived out some very beautiful but also painful experiences did the answer wash over me in loving waves. Knowing who we are and who we are created to be can take a lifetime to answer, but it doesn't have to. The question itself is a journey, and the answer can change as we change. Sometimes the depth of this question takes us to a place we don't want to go, and we fight the raw edge of panic that steals our breath away. Sometimes the answers unfurl without us being conscious of it. But you might be asking, why should we care about answering this question? Remember, even Jesus asked his disciples "Who do you say that I am?" (Matthew 16:15).

The first person we make a home with is ourselves. The first person we befriend is ourselves. In befriending ourselves, we become hospitable to God, who makes a home in us. In knowing more about who we are, we can know more of who God is and his plan for our lives. Striving to understand who we are is not selfish but an act of courage and love. In learning to be at home with ourselves, we can help others make a home in themselves. As the old maxim goes: "Be yourself; everyone else is already taken."

This is our starting place, so take a deep breath as we take the next steps in our journey together.

Take a Deep Breath

Each of us has our essential nature and "spirit"—the essence of what makes us who we are. I see it today with my own children: they are born with their own spirit that is somewhat shaped by us as their parents but that largely comes from within. It is something intangible, ethereal, otherworldly. It is not simply a light in our minds or a fire in our hearts but a spark from deep within, at the core of our existence. We did not light it ourselves, so where does it come from?

Our spirit did not generate itself; neither did we create it. It comes from a Divine Being who has breathed life into you and me, into all of us. I call this being God, and it is out of God's love that we are born. It is this love that is at the core of our being. This spirit is the Divine Love that lives within each of us.

Through trial and triumph this love may strengthen or diminish, but we cannot deny that it is there. The soul is the inner sanctuary of God's incarnated presence within us. Each of us feels something in our own way. To be a human being is to have a soul, and to have a soul is to be a spiritual person. Maybe you haven't thought about this before, that God breathes his life into each of us. But he does—a spark of divine breath that comes from the one who animates us and gives us life. In fact, the ancient Greek word for spirit is *pneuma*, which means "breath." You and I are filled with *divine* air. The breath of God not just moves within us but stirs all around us. Rather than painfully holding our breath through life, we need to be conscious of and open to this presence. A prayer written by Edwin Hatch and based on the prayer and hymn of St. Columba speaks specifically of this breath of God that can fill our lives if we unite ourselves to him:

O breathe on me,
O breath of God, fill me with life anew,
that I may love the things you love,
and do what you would do.
O breathe on me, O breath of God,
until my heart is pure;
until my will is one with yours,
to do and to endure.
O breathe on me, O breath of God,
my will to yours incline,
until this selfish part of me
glows with Your fire divine.
O breathe on me, O breath of God,
so I shall never die,
but live with you the perfect life
for all eternity.

This breath of God unites us in spirit. Today, many people, especially young people, have at best an ambivalent attitude toward religion and at worst a negative posture toward religion and religious people. But when we think about spirituality, people generally seem to have a far more positive view. Part of the reason for this is that religion in the mainstream media is often equated with rigidity, hypocrisy, and being old-fashioned. It is trendier to say that you are "spiritual but not religious" because *religion* means identification with a particular religious tradition. Religion is often seen as a binary, didactic system of thought that is incapable of flexing to accommodate messiness and brokenness. Yet the word *religion* comes from the Latin *ligare*, which means "to knit or to bind together." What has been bound up together? It is our body, mind, and soul—and their relationship to one another and ultimately to the animating principle who created us.

Your spirit is your soul spark.

Soul Spark

The soul is the cavern of eternal memory. It is the part of us that lives beyond our physical death. The *Catechism of the Catholic Church*, among the definitive sources of the Catholic Church's tradition, "teaches that every spiritual soul is created immediately by God—it is not 'produced' by the parents—and that it is immortal: it does not perish when it separates from the body at death, and it will be reunited with the body at the final Resurrection" (*CCC*, #366). Your soul, then, is the spark of God's immortal love within you.

In Ireland, when someone has gone through a particularly difficult experience, we often say "they have lost their soul." They have been "dispirited," or their spirit has diminished, to use a term that we don't hear very often anymore. They acknowledge that something is missing; a light has been dimmed, their soul is dispirited and separated. For example, my friend Billy has struggled with low self-esteem for years, and one day I asked him, "When was the last time you felt truly happy and at peace?" He responded, "When I was eight." That was forty years ago for Billy. How long ago was that for you? The weight of life can be crushing at times, but it can also be punctuated with times of intense joy and immense gratitude. In the rush of life and the midst of distractions, we may have forgotten how to be carefree, to be truly happy and at peace. We have forgotten how to converse with our own soul and the wisdom it imparts to us.

Today we often use the expression "old soul" to describe someone who seems wise beyond their years. Old souls are people of incredible depth who are empathetic, quietly attuned, and highly aware of the world around them. They possess an inner light and are deeply spiritual people. People around them can sense that a great lake of wisdom resides in the depths of their souls, a wisdom that transcends time.

Old soul or not, to be a human being is to have a spirituality whether or not we consciously live out of that spirituality and nurture this relationship with the divine. In general, spirituality refers to how humans experience and nurture their relationship with their creator, God. Christian spirituality relates to God in and through Jesus Christ. When it is actively pursued, spirituality is a path to wholeness or, to put it another way, to holiness. Religion is how we worship and express our relationship to God, and this should bring us joy, peace, and wholeness, not weariness, guilt, and shame.

We humans sometimes forget the core of who we are and who we are created to be. The more we get closer to breaking open that core of who we are, the better our relationships are, the healthier we feel, and life becomes a place where we truly thrive and not just survive. So, how do we get to the core? Let's take a step closer.

Getting to the Core

We all want to be known and loved. Never once have I met a person who did not want to receive more love, to be loved with complete understanding and acceptance. This is possible when we embrace the core of who we are, created in relationship to God, who is love. We can either accept God's love or move away from it. As a result, during particularly tough times in our life we often vacillate between falling apart and breaking open. Falling apart and breaking open might at first seem to be a lot alike, but there are differences. Let's explore this by using a very unspiritual metaphor here to help us, one drawn from the principles of physics.

Most of us have heard of the concept of centrifugal force, coined by Christiaan Huygens in his 1659 work *De vi centrifuga*. Centrifugal force causes an object moving in a circular path to be flung out and away from the center of its path. This path takes place along the radius of a circle from the center out toward the object. When apart from that center, the object destabilizes, splits, and falls apart. It is often unrecognizable from the central principle the farther from the core that it travels.

Let me give you another analogy here that might help: the Tilt-A-Whirl at an amusement park. That's the ride that spins and spins faster and faster as it moves round and round. This ride uses the principle of centrifugal force to generate momentum, and it can make your head spin! If you go on this ride, you are advised not to have any loose objects on you because when you're spinning, all of those objects, like the loose coins in your pocket, will be flung away from you and get lost. Some people feel exhilarated by this process, but others feel disoriented.

This principle of centrifugal force applies not just to inanimate objects but to each of us on our spiritual journey. When we move away from the center or core of who we are called to be, sometimes by our own choices, sometimes by circumstance, we spin and spin, and the pain can cause us to fall apart, to shatter into what feels like a million pieces. The current pace of life largely emphasizes frenetic activity and rapidity. But activity begets activity, and the more we do, the faster life spins and the more life blurs before us, just as if we were on a Tilt-A-Whirl. All the loose edges of our pain, our relationships, and our experiences fall apart from us on the Tilt-A-Whirl of life. We feel pulled away from the core of who we are, and we begin to lose our own voice. We become dark and the world seems dark. We no longer can hear the inner voice of love urging us to slow down and take a time-out. This is what I mean by falling apart.

If you read the Bible, you will find plenty of people and relationships that fall apart—Adam and Eve and Cain and Abel, for example. You will also find numerous examples of people who fall down and in their brokenness are opened up to the grace of God—people like the Samaritan woman, Mary Magdalene, St. Paul, Peter, and others. Jesus himself was broken open for us in his life, death, and resurrection. In the Scriptures we read that Jesus breaks the bread (1 Corinthians 11:24) and shares it with his disciples. The bread doesn't fall apart but is broken open by Jesus' own hands and becomes the "bread of life" (John 6:35) for his followers. Today at Mass we live this out: the bread is broken open by the priest and shared with those who are present. We all share in the breaking of the bread, and this teaches us something very important spiritually: breaking open is always followed by transformation.

We are all broken in some way. But those of us who embrace our brokenness will be transformed.

In the breaking open of our fears, hopes, and joys, the real work of healing, finding acceptance, forgiving, and ultimately loving happens. This is the thin place where we meet God and our true selves. If we navigate the work of our breakdowns with thoughtfulness, openness, and faith, we might find that we can break through many of the forces that bind us. Breakdowns are often followed by breakthroughs, which can make our own experience of being broken open so much more powerful. That is one of the real differences between breaking open and falling apart: newness of life always follows when we break through and are broken open.

We cannot make this choice for others, only ourselves. But we can walk this same road together as pilgrims of the soul.

We Are a Pilgrim People

Brendan and I had been friends for two years before I had the courage to say to him, "Brendan, you do realize that what you do is not who you are?" "No, no, that's wrong Julianne," he said. "What I do is absolutely who I am, I'm defined by what I do," he reiterated. "Oh, Brendan, Brendan," I said as I shook my head, "you were made for far more than what you do."

Like a lot of people today, my dear friend Brendan truly believed that his worth was completely defined by what he did. Far too many of us define life by what we do and not who we are or who we are becoming. Let me tell you with every ounce of my Irish feistiness that *you are not just what you do!* What we work at or what we do has value, but our identity is not defined by the world or by the desires of the world. Our identity does not lie in our doing but in our *being*. Look, we are called human beings, not human doings, for a very good reason.

The French philosopher Gabriel Marcel proposed in his writings that the term *Homo sapiens* has been rendered obsolete in an age with such rapid technological and social advances. "Person with knowledge" or "wise person" seems to be a bit of a sparse description of the human person, in all fairness. "Wise person" is both inspirational and aspirational but also not realistic at the best of times. Instead, Marcel proposes that we replace the term *Homo sapiens* with *Homo viator*, which means "a being on the way," much like a pilgrim.

To see ourselves as pilgrim beings is not merely to recognize and accept our existence but to recognize the givenness of our existence. We are neither the center nor the origin of our own existence because there is a very definite light that illuminates and guides us on our way. It is our relationship with this light—God—who gifts us with presence instead of void, meaning instead of nothingness, and hope instead of despair.

We are beings on the way, then, part of a "great cloud of witnesses" (Hebrews 12:1) on the road of life together, united in a spiritual journey. Within each of us is a sacred mystery that we must honor and acknowledge as we journey together. Each of us carries wounds that can make us better or bitter, depending on whether we accept our wounds as blessing or burden. I have heard people say that "pain that is not transformed but is transferred" or more simply that "hurting people hurt others." Pain always transforms us, but it can also transfigure us. The word *transfigure* means to illuminate or elevate through a transformation so that a person becomes radiant. It comes from the Latin word *transfigurare*, which means "to change the shape of." The term is most closely associated with the transfiguration of Jesus, which is found in the Synoptic Gospels of Matthew, Mark, and Luke. We can become transfigured in light through our suffering and pain, and that pain will change us so that we can let more light into our hearts. But if we continually identify ourselves solely with hurt, we will live out of that hurt and become hurtful. If we draw from the well of love within, we become a well of love to others, a well that will not run dry because love begets love and goodness begets goodness.

We are a pilgrim people. Your pilgrim road might be cobbled and worn or it might be full of potholes, sinkholes, or broken concrete, but all of us walk this pilgrim road together.

On this pilgrim road, believe that . . .

> Who you are is enough.
> You carry the spark of divine love within you.
> You are loved just as you are.
> You are a gift.
> You matter.
> You are precious.
> You are a beloved child of God.

We have taken a few important steps on our journey together. We all are walking this pilgrim road together as we cross from the known to the unknown, from the place of fear to a place of love. We are journeying into thin space. So, in the next chapter, let's explore this little thing that is actually a really big thing called fear.

Your Thin Place: Who Are You?

Breaking Open
Irish seanfhocal (old word): Bíonn gach
tosach lag.
Translation: Every beginning is weak.

As you begin your journey of discovering, rediscovering, or perhaps uncovering who you are, the Irish *seanfhocal* reminds us that the first draft of our thoughts is often the hardest. Every beginning may be tentative as you set out on your journey, but it will get better and stronger as you walk the road ahead. Take heart, and as we say in Ireland, *tóg go bog é*, which means "take it easy" on yourself.

Breaking Through
- How do you feel about entering a thin space?
- How would you answer the question, Who are you? What are some of the attributes and characteristics that you would sketch out?
- Name three or four practices or ideas that you feel have pulled you away from who you were created to be.
- Name three or four practices that have strengthened your core.

Breaking Free
Before I formed you in the womb, I knew you.

—Jeremiah 1:15

God knows each of us intimately and is at the deepest core of who we are. He knows our faults and failings yet loves us anyway. Take a few minutes today to speak to God by reflecting on the question, Who are you? Share your thoughts and give this "thin time" to God.

2

Facing Our Fears

Irish seanfhocal (old word): An rud a ghoilleas
ar an gcroí caithfidh an t-súil é a shileas.
Translation: What pains the heart must be
washed away with tears.

Like most young people growing up in Ireland during the 1990s, I didn't think much about faith and religion, although they were all around me. It was out of a sense of obligation rather than love that I went to Mass, and not once do I remember my parents praying with me out loud or referencing the Bible, never mind reading it. I went to Mass each week, sometimes with my parents, sometimes on my own, but Mass was much more of a social outing than any kind of spiritual nourishment. So it was quite a surprise when, at the age of sixteen, I experienced what is called a *metanoia* (a conversion of heart and mind) on a school field trip or, rather, a pilgrimage, to "Ireland's holiest mountain" in County Mayo.

Meeting Patrick on Pilgrimage

Pilgrimage has always been a sacred practice of prayer and transformation in many cultures, including for the Irish. Rugged and imposing, Croagh Patrick (taken from the Irish words *Cruach Phadraig*, meaning "Patrick's stack") has been a site of pilgrimage for three thousand years. Nicknamed "The Reek" by locals, one million people climb

Croagh Patrick annually, and the numbers continue to rise. The reasons for climbing are many and varied. Some climb for exercise and fun, others to atone for a wrongdoing, and still others make the grueling climb to search for meaning, as people have done for thousands of years or to grow closer to God. My motivation to climb the mountain had little to do with undertaking a spiritual journey. I was driven more by a sense of adventure and the promise of having a giant sleepover with the girls in my class. With Mrs. Dorothy, our religion teacher, twenty-three giggling girls boarded a train to the west of Ireland and settled in for what I thought would be a weekend of merriment and mischief. We began our climb on a bright Saturday morning and met with Father Frank Fahey, our pilgrimage guide. Right away, Father Frank talked to us about the difference between a trip and a pilgrimage: the former is more of a surface engagement with your surroundings, whereas the latter is designed to experience inner change and transformation. For many people, pilgrimages can be supercharged thin-place experiences.

Father Frank was parish priest of Ballintubber Abbey, located in the town of Ballintubber or, to use the Irish name for the town, *Baile an Tobair Phádraig*, meaning "the place of St. Patrick's well." This town traces its origins to the time when St. Patrick baptized the villagers around the year AD 440. This was all ancient history to me! But my curiosity was piqued by Father Frank's familiarity and apparent friendship with St. Patrick and the God that St. Patrick loved. I could not have had a better and more knowledgeable guide to Celtic spirituality and to pilgrimage than Father Frank.

In high spirits but a wee bit sleepy, our group set off on the Tóchar Phádraig, (the "way of Patrick"), following the same ancient route that St. Patrick had apparently taken. It was on this route that I learned an important lesson from St. Patrick in facing our fears and conquering our demons. This lesson has stayed with me ever since, giving me the strength to overcome my fears and to persist in conquering those demons that try to imprison me or hold me back. So, let's step back about 1,600 years to ancient Ireland to meet St. Patrick on a mountainous pilgrimage and see what lessons he has in store for us.

Climbing a Mountain of Fear

By all accounts, St. Patrick is an enigma. Beyond the stories and legends of him, we are unsure of his date or place of birth. We are unsure of the exact routes by which St. Patrick traversed the countryside of Ireland. Little is known about his life, and yet he lives on in popular culture as the man who drove the snakes out of Ireland and explained the Trinity using a shamrock. What we are sure of can be found in his writings, *The Confessio*, or *The Confessions*, in which his humility, strength of faith, and utter devotion to Our Lord is revealed.

After being captured as a child by Irish pirates in Roman Britain and enslaved on a mountain called *Slieve Mish* or *Slemish*, Patrick dramatically escapes and returns home. To his family's dismay, he leaves once again to train for the priesthood, inspired by having heard God's voice during his captivity. After being appointed a bishop, Patrick is sent back to Ireland to preach the Gospel to the native Irish, who are renowned for their pagan ways. He spends forty days and forty nights on Croagh Patrick to prepare for his public ministry, knowing that the site is sacred to the Irish, particularly to the pagan Druids. Patrick sets out to claim the mountain for Christ and in doing so faces down his fears and demons.

Folklore tells us that Patrick carried two items on his journey up the mountain: his crozier (a hooked staff carried by a bishop as a symbol of authority) and a bell that functioned as a sort of alert to announce his presence and call people to prayer. As he was climbing the mountain, hosts of blackbirds swirled around St. Patrick. He had been fasting, so he was tired and hungry. The blackbirds persisted in pecking him and tormented him with their shrieks. Patrick rang his prayer bell vigorously to scatter the birds and be relieved of their incessant cries. This pattern was repeated several times. Eventually Patrick managed to banish the blackbirds forever. The great St. Patrick's "Clog" (bell) that is on display in the National Museum of Ireland is reputed to have turned black from the constant barrage of attacks on St. Patrick.

Once he got to the summit of the mountain, no doubt feeling a great sense of accomplishment at making it to the top, a surprise awaited St. Patrick. A mighty serpent slithered close to him, and this being an Irish tale, of course the serpent could speak! When Patrick asked the creature to identify itself, the serpent named herself as the mother of the devil, the *Caoránach* in the Irish language. Without hesitation, Patrick took his crozier and gave her an "almighty whack," as the Irish say! He didn't kill the creature, but it slithered off to a lake and remained there. To this day the lake is known as *Loch na Peiste*, or "the lake of the serpent."

What, you may ask, is the meaning behind this strange tale? The legend of St. Patrick, Father Frank reminded me, is as powerful today as it was 1,600 years ago. It is not just a tale of adventure; it is primarily a spiritual metaphor for breaking down our fears and moving into thin space. Let's take a look.

Conquering Your Demons and Ego

Just like physically climbing a mountain, every time we set out to attain a goal, whether striving for a better life, pursuing additional education, or bettering ourselves, demons will attack us—from within and without. These metaphorical demons—doubts, imperfections, feelings of unworthiness, weaknesses of mind and body—represent the spiritual struggles we must engage in to break down and face our fears. The blackbirds that attacked Patrick gnawed at his peace and happiness. It was only by persistently ringing his prayer bell that he was able to banish and scatter them. The demons that harangue us often visit in the form of an inner voice that whispers, and sometimes screams, repeatedly, "You cannot do this, you are not good enough." We listen to them, and if we believe them, they prevent us from having the courage to keep climbing.

Sometimes those demons come in the form of uncertainties from others who tell us that we are not qualified enough, special enough, or accomplished enough to climb whatever mountain we set out to climb. It is only through focus and prayer that we keep our attention on maintaining our core and thus conquer those demons. And just when we think we are truly ready to set out on our mission, the greatest demon of all comes to tempt us. What gives birth to evil (represented by the serpent in the story) is our own ego or our pride. Our ego often manifests itself in our desire to play God with our own life or the lives of others. The letters *EGO* stand for "edging God out," my friend Lisa reminds me. Ego came to Patrick in the guise of a serpent and represented the pride and anger that we all harbor within.

Patrick reminds us that we cannot kill our own pride or anger but must work on them relentlessly. Like the screeching blackbirds, it is the demons of fear and doubt that chip away at our sense of peace and joy, and it is often our own ego that stands in the way of true fulfillment and contentment. During this time, I realized that Patrick's story is the story of all of us. At its heart lies the universal truth that if we do not conquer doubt and fear, we will succumb to ego, our own comfort, and eventually despair.

It was this story that settled into my bones with every step as I climbed Croagh Patrick. As the climb toward the top became more challenging, I began to understand how fear and doubt can imprison and paralyze us. As I suffered through blistered feet and biting flies

(I counted twenty-eight welts on my face alone after the climb!), I sat on the top of the mountain and wept at the sheer magnificence of the world around me. My soul sent up what was perhaps my first open-hearted prayer to God, a prayer of thanksgiving—for the beauty of the world, for every human being, and for my own life. At that moment, I felt my soul expand with love, and in my openness, I received a new perspective.

Sitting on the damp grass, watching the drumlins (small islands) of Clew Bay beneath me, I had a thought that was, I believe, a response to the gratitude of my heart. The sun rises and sets every day whether we see it or not. The fact that we don't see it doesn't change the truth of this event. God's love is the same. It rises like the sun each day for us whether we recognize it or not, whether we accept that love or reject it. And it was in that moment I gave my heart over to God. "Send me wherever you will, God," I whispered. "Like the sun, guide my next steps, I will trust you," I said, and yet I was afraid—afraid to deal with my "junk."

What's in Your Junk Drawer?

Like most people, I have a junk drawer in my house. This is the place where I stuff all the unwanted things that I don't want to deal with: batteries, paperclips, pencils, odd notepads, rubber bands, and all kinds of odds and ends. Crap—but crap that I cannot seem to throw away. Everybody in the house seems to instinctively know where this drawer is and adds their own stash to it. Some of us have a junk drawer or a whole room and even a dedicated place like a storage unit where we stash the things that we don't know what to do with. Sound familiar? Junk drawers are generally places that we like to keep hidden from others. We are forced to sort through this junk drawer when it is too full to hold anything more or when there is one item that continues to get stuck over and over until we have no choice but to deal with it. Like the potato masher in the drawer that keeps popping up and jamming the drawer. It doesn't belong there, but we are too stubborn to put it somewhere else, so we push it in to make it fit!

We tiptoe around having to deal with the junk drawer, and so it gets more and more cluttered through the years. That's how junk drawers procreate and multiply. When the drawer is full, sometimes we "sort it out," but most of the time we move along to another spot that becomes an overflow junk drawer, and then we have not one but two junk drawers to deal with!

In our heart too, we have a junk drawer. It is the shadow place in our soul where we stuff all our hurts, shame, guilt, and denials so that we don't have to deal with them. Taking the time to sort through these experiences would be too difficult, so instead we adopt an "out of sight, out of mind" approach and shut them away. But of course, they linger because "out of sight, out of mind" does not mean "out of heart, out of soul."

It's important to note that not everything in our heart junk drawer was put there by us. Our hearts gather up fear and shame from our family, from other people, and from events over which we sometimes have no control. That cluttered and frightening inner drawer contains fragments of family history and emotional or spiritual habits we learned from people around us.

How we choose to deal with what's in there is a story all its own. The unkind words hurled at us in an argument, the acne scars left behind to remind us of those awkward teenage years, the divorce that shattered our self-image, or the shame of abuse are all buried in the hidden places of our hearts. We know they are there, but we continue to push them away. So, what do we do? Sometimes we shop too much or eat and drink too much to soothe and numb the raw edges of pain stirred by our memories. Some of us ignore these wounds until they bubble up unexpectedly and cause us to question our very existence.

Some of us fixate on those wounds and continue to put more and more into our junk drawer until just the sight of it causes our heart to sink and our blood pressure to rise. It has often happened to me that I can get the drawer open only a crack before it jams up, so I rattle and rattle it, hoping that the contents will settle just enough so that I can peek inside. That darned potato masher has popped up once again!

But we can ignore an eyesore for only so long before it becomes a heartsore and, more deeply, a soulsore. Even though we know at some point that we have to open it, why do we keep this drawer hidden? One word: fear.

FEAR: Face Everything and Rise

The junk drawer in our hearts is a place of fear. The deepest fear at the heart of who we are is that if we share this place with others, they will love us less. We will be rejected and abandoned.

In that hidden place certain questions are longing for a voice: If people knew who I really was deep down, would I still be loved? Can I ever be truly vulnerable with another person? If I make a huge mistake, is my life defined by that experience? If these are some of your questions, then you are not alone.

How each of us chooses to cope with what is kept in our junk drawer tells a lot about our approach to life. We embrace or eliminate, avoid or accept. Exploring who we really are means looking at the entirety of our strengths and weaknesses. Most of the time it's easier to focus on our strengths, but this is not entirely honest, because it is in our weaknesses that we are purified and strengthened. It is in being vulnerable that we are the most brave and courageous. We can never outrun or hide from our weaknesses. Like the potato masher in the drawer, trust me, your weaknesses and failures will pop up when you least expect it! As my aunt used to say to me, "When you sweep so much dirt under the carpet, one day you will trip over it."

The mystery at the heart of our being is that it is our weaknesses and our vulnerabilities that are touchstones of grace for ourselves and for others—if only we have the courage to face them.

My husband has for a number of years worked with those who have addictions, particularly alcohol addiction. He once said to me that in terms of addictions, they are "less about what we are consuming and more about what is consuming us." A wise friend of mine summed up his journey of addiction as follows:

> The person takes a drink.
> The drink takes a drink.
> The drink takes the person.
> Or to put it another way:
> I take a drink.
> My thirst for a drink takes a drink.
> Eventually the drink takes over my life.

There is nothing inherently wrong with enjoying alcohol in moderation. But as the second statement above highlights, it's when we drink to quench a thirst fueled by insatiable needs that problems can develop. It's not just about what we are drinking or eating but what is also eating away at us, physically, emotionally, mentally, and spiritually. Maybe it isn't drinking for you, but your busyness, or your shopping habit, your social media usage, or food. It's not what we are drinking but what's drinking away our peace and joy. It is not what we are buying but what is stealing away our time and energy. These are the forces that continue to pull us away from our core.

It's time to ask yourself, What is in that hidden place, the junk drawer, that eats away at my sense of peace and happiness? What's consuming me from the inside out? And then it's time to face those fears.

If the thought of going into your junk drawer scares you, well, you are not alone. Opening it takes tremendous courage, but we must do it in order to live a whole and holy life. It is necessary to cross into thin space. When we lay bare our weaknesses before God and break them down with time, prayer, and reflection, we emerge stronger.

Jesus reminds us of this difficult work as people of faith when he tells us, "My grace is sufficient for you, for power is made perfect in weakness . . . for whenever I am weak, then I am strong (2 Corinthians 12:9–11). Working on our weaknesses is a real lesson in humility, trust, and faith in the way that removing the crap from our junk drawer leaves opportunities for more meaningful people, experiences, and lessons to fill the space instead. To use a simple analogy, imagine that you are holding lots of shopping bags in your hands, so many in fact, that you do not have a free hand to spare. Someone comes and offers you a gift. But you cannot accept that gift because your hands are full. What must you do? You need to set down your bags so that you can accept the gift.

We all want the junk drawer of our heart to be a place of peace and compassion, for ourselves and for others. If we can make peace with the shadow, we learn to live in the light and be a light for others. If we do not, our demons will haunt us relentlessly. We can face our fears and overcome them, or else they will consume us, just as St. Patrick reminds us. On the day that Sister Anne asked me, "Who are you?" I opened the junk drawer of my heart partway and shared with her the pain that I normally kept hidden. It was terrifying and painful because when we open up our heart-drawers, we feel vulnerable and exposed.

God wants to do the same for us. He wants us to clear out our junk drawers so that we can receive new gifts of life.

Name and Shame

Opening our junk drawers can be a painful return to some of the most difficult experiences in our lives. For me, it was specific moments and experiences in my childhood and teenage years that culminated with my deciding to leave Ireland. It seemed easier at the time to start afresh and to work through my pain alone than with the people and the experiences that had caused the pain. In opening my drawer, I had to pinpoint exactly what was in the drawer, who put it there, and how it was put there. There were times when the anxiety I felt inside bubbled up and gripped my chest, but just like Patrick, I kept on climbing that mountain one step at a time by breaking down my fear. One of the biggest steps you can take on your journey is to name what or who it is that shames you and any residual guilt you may feel.

Shame and guilt, while connected, are not the same. Guilt is often an emotion that arises as a result of a behavior or activity. Shame is connected to your deepest identity and focused not just on the behavior or event but on your *self*. Guilt says, "What happened was bad," whereas shame says, "You are bad." At the heart of shame is the lie that you are unlovable, worthless, stupid, or useless. One of my favorite passages in Scripture comes from Isaiah 43:1 and says, "Do not fear, for I have redeemed you; I have called you by name; you are mine." God will always call you out of love. Evil, by contrast, will always call you by your shame. "Liar," "thief," "bad mother," "absent father," "junkie," "alcoholic"—shame whispers repeatedly until it breaks you down and sometimes you believe the lie even though you shouldn't.

Shame rewrites the narrative about your potential and who you are created to be. Repetition is its currency. In the absence of support, love, and encouragement, shame can get a foothold in our lives and hold us back physically, emotionally, spiritually, and mentally as we try to climb whatever mountain we have set our heart on. Shame will use whatever it can to twist the inner voice of love to the negative.

"You don't deserve to be happy!" it shouts. "Don't enjoy this too much, it won't last," or the familiar "Wait until they find out who you *really* are"—it repeats over and over. Time to shut it down, ladies and gentlemen! Make the decision to end shame's power over you right now, and the release you feel will wash over you in waves. If you have a trusted friend, a spiritual director, or a counselor who is walking with you, feel free to break down the contents of your junk drawer with that person by your side. If you are too scared to talk, write it down, reach out, or find a way to release the hold these experiences have over you. Clear out that junk drawer once and for all!

We all go through tough times, experience suffering, and make mistakes. Some of those mistakes are terrible or seem irredeemable. We think we are ruined or tainted. Not so. When light and dark come together, something new and beautiful is always created. And the same is true in the ordinariness of life. When we break something like a plate or a teacup, we often cannot find a use for it any longer and regretfully throw the object away. But there is a practice in the Japanese culture called *kintsugi* (金継ぎ), literally "golden" and "repair," that teaches us to accept our mistakes and failures as the means of transformation.

The practice of *kintsugi* takes broken objects and repairs them with precious liquid gold, silver, or lacquer and dusts them with powdered gold. Each object that cracks or breaks does so in unique ways, and in the repair of the object, the breaks are not hidden or covered up but instead are highlighted. The cracks and scars are gilded and create a piece of art, far more beautiful than the original. In this, beauty replaces uniformity.

Throughout our lives, we crack and break open. Sometimes we try and put the pieces back together ourselves by hiding the cracks and scars that we bear. If we do not learn to accept where those fault lines lie, in time, the seams will open once more and we will fall apart.

But in breaking open and making ourselves authentically available to God, something beautiful happens. We enter thin space. God meets us in the cracking open. He doesn't gloss over our cracks but instead guides us in the repair process so that our cracks turn into golden scars that we bear, not with shame, but with love and acceptance.

And this teaches us another valuable lesson. We cannot be available to God and others if we sit inert, mourning our failures and cracks. The essence of resilience and beauty is found in all our experiences, not just the good ones, the perfect ones, the untainted ones. But especially in the experiences where we have been broken open and the golden light of love knits us back together, imperfectly perfect just as God designed us to be.

In this thin space, God invites us to make ourselves available to him and offer up all that we are to the master craftsman, who wants to transform us through our sufferings and failings. It is not in perfection that we are made great, it is in our imperfections, as God tells us: "My grace is sufficient for you, for my power is made perfect in weakness" (2 Corinthians 12:9).

Let's keep working through this together, taking it a step at a time. Breaking down and naming shame is the first step in breaking its hold on you. It's the first step, but not the only step, in breaking open and rising to a new identity and fresh start. But it is one of the most powerful ways that you can open the junk drawer, break down what is inside, and enter into thin space. From there, you can begin to put the pieces together and see what fits or what you reject. One day at a time, one step at a time. Now that we have a good start in working through who we are and dealing with our junk, let's move to the next step of breaking down what holds us back.

Your Thin Place: Facing Our Fears

Breaking Open

Irish seanfhocal (old word): An rud a ghoilleas
ar an gcroí caithfidh an t-súil é a shileas.
Translation: What pains the heart must be
washed away with tears.

Letting your tears flow over a sorrow is not a sign of weakness but strength. The Irish expression *sileadh súl* literally means "draining an eye." Sometimes, the only way to drain the sorrow from the heart is through your tears and in the sweat of hard work.

Breaking Through

- What one memory, experience, feeling, or person would you remove from your secret, cluttered place? How might you go about cleaning out this drawer? Who can help?
- What is the "potato masher" that keeps popping up in your drawer that you are stubbornly clinging to?
- What are your "golden soul scars"? What do they look like? How have they been repaired?
- What has shame told you about who you are?
- What is the "lie" at the heart of your junk?

Breaking Free

"There is no fear in love. But perfect love drives out fear, because fear has to do with punishment. The one who fears is not made perfect in love" (1 John 4:18). This week, make a note of any incriminating thoughts that pass through your head, about yourself or others. Separate thoughts driven by fear from thoughts fueled by love. Where there is fear, put loving thoughts and intentions instead. As St. John of the Cross said, "Where there is no love, put love and you will draw out love."

3

The Darkness

*Irish seanfhocal (old word): Is doimhin é poll
an amhrais.
Translation: Deep is the hole of doubt.*

One of my favorite places in Ireland is the Boyne Valley, or what has
been referred to as Ireland's "Valley of the Kings." In this area there are
a number of megalithic tombs, the most famous being Newgrange,
which was built around 3200 BC, during the Neolithic period. This
makes Newgrange much older than Stonehenge and the Egyptian
pyramids. A UNESCO World Heritage Site, Newgrange consists of
a large circular mound with a stone passageway and chambers inside.
The mound has a retaining wall at the front and is ringed by "kerb-
stones" engraved with distinctive artwork. It is aligned with the rising
sun, and during the winter solstice, light floods the tomb and illuminates the inner chamber. For the Celts, this alignment with the winter sun must have been situated in the context of the interplay of the
light and the darkness.

Fire in Your Bones

The Celts were sun worshippers, and Bel and Lugh were among their
sun gods. The Celts marked time with fire as they celebrated their
gods at the festivals throughout the year such as Beltaine (around
April 30), Lughnasa (around August 1), the feast of Samhain

(October 31 or November 1), and Imbolc (February 1). As winter approached and the days shortened, the ancient Irish began to prepare for the food shortages that would undoubtedly come, as light waned and food became scarcer.

According to my friend and the Patrician scholar Father Frank Fahey, at an appointed time, the Celts would gather and drive their cattle off the cliffs of Ireland to kill the animals. The cattle were then butchered; the flesh was harvested and preserved for food and the skin for clothing; and every part of the animal was put to use. After the bones had been boiled for broth, they were gathered into a large pile and set on fire. The Celts set the bones on fire in thanksgiving for the lives of the cattle and to release the spirits of the cattle back into the world. These "bone fires" were always associated with the feast of Samhain and live on today in our Halloween bonfire. The "bone fire" is the origin of our bonfire!

Feeling the fire in our bones is part of our longing for something or someone more than who we are. Life is lived in the space between contradictions—a space where light does not contradict the darkness but coexists with it, where one enhances the other. We may think of darkness as the absence of light or light as the absence of darkness, but the reality is far more subtle. Physicists acknowledge that even though our photosensitive eyes may not be able to detect the presence of light in a dark room, for example, it does not mean that light is not there in some fashion. Within each of us, there is also an interplay of darkness and light, depending on how we navigate the shadows. Light and fire give warmth and heat. But light can also blind. Darkness can shroud us to provide cover to keep us safe, but if we dwell too much in the shadow of life, we can become invisible and live in fear. Shadows block light so that all we see is darkness just as our own struggles, weaknesses, and failings can hinder our ability to live in the light. This is not a new insight. Light and darkness are at the heart of life just as they have been for all cultures and many ancient civilizations such as the Celtic people.

We must see light and darkness not from a place of fear but from a place of love and growth, a place where the allure of sunlight is greater than living in a cave of our own darkness. And now, with that being said, there's a story I want to share with you about living in a cave.

The Cave of Darkness

Long ago, a group of prisoners were bound and chained from childhood at the bottom of a dark cave. With their legs and necks fixed and facing in one direction, all they could see was what was in front of them. The world that they interacted with was composed entirely of shadows projected on the wall by a fire that burned behind the prisoners. Within the cave, they heard noises and echoes of shadow people but were utterly convinced that what they saw in the shadows was in fact real and true.

What happens when one brave soul removes his chains and gets up the courage to walk toward the source of the shadows and into the light? With his heart in his mouth, he braves the darkness to walk from the bottom of the cave up to the light. Once he reaches the top of the cave, the light blinds him. His eyes have become so accustomed to the dark that this strange light is terrifying. At this stage, the darkness of the cave is preferable to the pain he is experiencing, but in time, his eyes adjust to the light so that he can see clearly. He realizes for the first time that this world of light is the real world, and the world inside the cave is but a pale imitation of this light-filled life. Instead of a fire being the source of light, he understands that the fire is in fact the sun. Excited to share this news with his friends, he descends into the darkness of the cave once again. Once again, his eyes take time to adjust from brightness to darkness, but his mind knows to expect it this time. After some time, he makes it to the bottom of the cave, where his friends are still sitting chained.

With great passion and excitement, he tells them about what he has seen and points out that the wall they are staring at is not real at all. There is a whole world behind them if they would just be brave enough to leave the darkness of the pit behind! He warns them about the blindness that he first experienced going from the dark into the light but shares that, just as his eyes did, their eyes will adjust. Instead of excitement and curiosity in their eyes, he sees fear and hostility. They wonder if the blindness he initially experienced has harmed him permanently. He is dejected and demoralized by their attitude and realizes that he has become an outsider forever. A line has been drawn. The prisoners make known their intent to kill him rather than leave the security of the cave and as such, it is the ending of something significant for both. The prisoners are no longer his friends, just as the bottom of the cave is no longer his home. He will never go back to pretend and live in darkness, and they will never have the courage to live in the light.

This two-thousand-year-old allegory is, of course, Plato's famous myth of the cave, which is detailed in book 7 of his masterpiece *The Republic*. The myth of the cave was written as a dialogue between Plato's brother Glaucon and his mentor Socrates, who narrates the tale and has many lessons for our own breaking through. Platonic scholars often tease out the epistemological (the theory of knowledge) or political elements of the myth of the cave. I want to look at the story through the lens of spirituality in the following paragraphs.

In the myth of the cave, Plato warns us against blindly accepting superficial reality and life at face value. Darkness engulfs the prisoners in the cave, who see shadows and half-truths as reality and truth. The chains that bind the prisoners would hardly be needed because they have so little desire to turn toward the light and uncover the truth about life and what it means for them. They are secure in their chains of darkness and comfort. But one decides to take a risk. For the one brave soul who leaves the cave, the bright light initially blinds and incapacitates him. But with time, the adjustment to reality comes, and he understands that his former home is a shadow of what life is supposed to be like.

The cave of darkness is prison, and the chains are fear. Armed with this understanding, this person realizes he has a responsibility to return to the cave, to help those who live in darkness come into the fullness of light, the fullness of life. Going back to the darkness again takes an adjustment, but with perseverance, the person keeps going until he reaches his friends. With great exuberance and excitement, he shares this life-transforming news. But instead of finding gratitude and curiosity, he encounters skepticism and suspicion.

Plato ends the tale with the caution that the prisoners, if they could, would rather kill this messenger of light than be dragged from the shadows of their life. The interplay between light and darkness is at the heart of Plato's myth of the cave. This allegory, which has survived across time and cultures, has deep insights for our work of breaking down our fears and leaning into truth. Let's uncover our own myth of the cave.

Light and Darkness

Light and darkness are the bookends of time.

The cooperation between light and darkness frames day and night, connects imagination and thought, bridges life and death. But light and darkness do not simply exist outside ourselves; they also reside within us. The journey from the darkness of the cave into the light of the sun mirrors our whole lives. I remember when I was expecting my first child and how I marveled that this child could grow in the darkness of the womb where seemingly light could not penetrate. The passage from the darkness of the womb was undoubtedly painful—I can feel the pains of childbirth to this day! The process of birth is its own transition, one from the darkness of the womb into the light of day. Darkness gives birth to light, and in death, the light fades as we close the eyes of our loved ones. We believe that death is complete darkness, the darkness of what we cannot see, but death is a movement of darkness giving way to eternal light.

And we are afraid of both. We are afraid of the light within ourselves but also of the darkness. We are equally afraid to shine and to stay in the shadows. We may be afraid to die but equally afraid to live. Within each of us lies a cavern of darkness, where we sit in the shadows of heartbreak and heartache. Like the old adage "birds of a feather, flock together"—or, as we say in Ireland, "where like finds like"—we find companions who also would rather sit in the shadows than confront the reality of light. But one day, we pluck up the courage to turn from our shadows and leave the darkness behind. As we emerge from our own prison or cave of thought, we are initially blinded by this new reality of light, and it hurts. Light illuminates all the shadows so that we can see into the dark corners of our soul. This is a painful process, and for a time we shrink from this light. But if we stand in this truth, we enter a thin space and begin to see more clearly than we ever have before.

Just like the prisoners chained in the cave, we can make company with thoughts, ideas, beliefs, prejudices, or people who chain us to look, feel, think, or act a certain way. Our soul can become a place that lives only in shadow. That is, until we decide to break free and move toward the inner light of our own soul, the place where goodness resides, the space where God is waiting for us. Unlike humanity, where light and darkness reside in equal measure, God "is light; in him there is no darkness at all" (1 John 1:5). Part of our journey as people of faith is to continue to walk toward the pure light of God's love.

As we leave the darkness of old ways of being, or what we call sin in the Christian tradition, the light can hurt and even blind us. We wonder whether it is easier to live in the darkness and cave of fear rather than stand in the light. Our old habits and behaviors are familiar and safe even if they hurt and imprison us. For a time, we waver on the threshold of the old and the new. But with courage and the gift of time, we adjust and move from the old way of being, to a new way of seeing. We then realize that a great responsibility has been laid upon us: we must turn back and descend into the cave to confront the darkness that's waiting. Again, we go through an adjustment, thinking, "Do I really want to go back to that place?" but knowing that if we do not, the darkness will haunt us. Often this experience is one of the most painful thresholds that we must cross. But we do not cross this threshold alone. If we call upon God, he will walk with us—and carry us if needed—through this journey.

So, we descend into the cave and find our old sins and fears waiting for us. With God's grace we confront them and our own reasons for their attraction and entombment. Unless we walk away from them, they will still try to chain us to a wall or worse yet, kill us, often slowly and unexpectedly. Hopefully we realize that this choice is no choice at all and so walk again into the light. While we know that the cave is still there, it has no hold on us anymore. We stand instead in the truth of our own light, having faced our fears. We live in hope instead of despair. We try to avoid the darkness of sin as we seek the light.

Death by Despair and the Inner Work of the Cave

Far from being a singular or individual task, the facing of fear is something for the collective. It is not just something for "me" but for "we." As a culture, we are quite good at masking, denying, or drowning in the shadow caves of despair, a picture painted very well by recent research on the main causes of death within the United States.

The phrase "deaths of despair" or "diseases of despair" comes from the groundbreaking work of economists Anne Case and Sir Angus Deaton. A 2015 paper entitled "Rising Morbidity and Mortality in Midlife among White Non-Hispanic Americans in the 21st Century" revealed a startling increase in midlife mortality among that demographic group. Since 2005, many leading causes of death, including stroke, cancer, heart disease, and lung disease, have all been decreasing. But deaths from drugs, alcohol, and suicide—what some call "deaths of despair"—have been steadily on the rise.

Various research studies confirm that younger Americans in general are particularly affected by despair. According to reports released by the public-health groups Trust for America's Health and Well Being Trust, between 2007 and 2017, drug-related deaths increased by 108 percent among adults ages 18 to 34, while alcohol-related deaths increased by 69 percent and suicides increased by 35 percent, according to the report, which drew on data from the Centers for Disease Control and Prevention. On the whole, about thirty-six thousand millennials died "deaths of despair" in 2017, with fatal drug overdoses being the biggest driver.

Various panels and institutes across the country have gathered to examine this phenomenon of deaths of despair, including faculty and students from the Department of Global Health and Population (GHP) at Harvard's T. H. Chan School of Public Health, which delved into the potential causes of this type of death at an event on November 18, 2019. Many scholars there argued that such deaths are the result of deep structural, economic, and social issues in American society. All undoubtedly true. But often omitted from the conversation is the topic of spirituality, the essence of what ties each of us together: body, mind, and soul.

Spirit can by nourished only by spirit. When we try to fuel our immaterial spirits with material things, we are left feeling unsatisfied, hungry, and dull. Immaterial souls can never be nourished by material things. It is clear that many people, including our loved ones and even ourselves, have drowned or are continuing to drown in a cave of despair filled with alcohol, drugs, and the absence of spirituality. If our world continues to focus only on the material and not the spiritual, it is likely that we will see deaths of despair continuing to rise. If spirituality is a way for us to live out what we most value—our relationship with God and with others—it is the seam that connects us all as humanity. What will it take for us to leave this cave and walk toward the light, individually and as a society? Economic and social factors are a huge part of the answer. But unless we position spirituality as a major contributor to the conversation, the answers will come in the form of plans, policies, and procedures instead of the real work that comes with inspiring of hope or wholeness—or holiness.

If we ignore spirituality in this chapter of America's history, we will have a much more luxurious cave filled with better-quality things and more courteous and well-mannered companions, but we will still live in a cave. Each of us has a spirit, and unless we talk about what crushes our spirit, we will never allow the light of spirituality to penetrate the darkness of the world.

Pope Francis, leader of 1.2 billion Catholics in the world, said something particularly profound in regard to our culture. "Sooner or later, we have to face our true selves and let the Lord enter. This may not happen unless we see ourselves staring into the abyss of a frightful temptation, or have the dizzying sensation of standing on the precipice of utter despair, or find ourselves completely alone and abandoned" (*Gaudete et Exultate*, no. 29). During the COVID-19 pandemic, many of us realized that what we missed most was not the shopping mall or ease of travel but people and experiences.

Consider Olivia. Olivia has been friends with a group of ladies since high school, and every year they go on a girls' weekend together. As they have grown older, the topics have changed from dating to marriage, and then to raising children and caring for aging parents. Even though these women have known one another for more than twenty years, they talk about their lives in two-dimensional form: there is length and height to their conversation but little depth. "We all know it," Olivia shared with me. "We talk on the surface level because we know that if we scratch that surface, the hurts that tumble out might take us to a place we aren't ready to deal with." But Olivia was tired of pretending that "things were just fine" and decided on the next girls' weekend in Nashville to broach the subject of going deeper. At one point, she talked about the pain of her divorce and how it had affected her core, her spiritual life.

What happened next was astounding: Olivia's friends all opened up to one another on a deeper level than ever. Olivia's vulnerability empowered the other women to own their own pain and put their struggles on the table. "We have a shared story in our pain and sadness but also a desire to really talk about our spirituality and what God is doing in our lives. We don't all use the same words, but we finally had a conversation without pretending," Olivia said. Through that weekend, the women found that they went from a two-dimensional conversation to a three-dimensional one, with added depth. It was a conversation that united them as they shared what was happening at the soul level. The bonds between them all became stronger as they loosened the bonds of silence in sharing their pain. It is a lesson for all of us.

Emerging from Our Cocoon

We can ignore the gnawing pain at the edge of our soul for only so long before it starts consuming us from the inside out. This is an emptiness beyond the reach of anything we can humanly fill it with. Nothing we can buy, eat, drink, or do can appease this ache. But it comes to us in the form of relationship.

For centuries, people from all walks of life and all cultures have found great peace and strength in a relationship with God. It is in this relationship that we find the courage to leave behind old ways of being and step into the light. This is the great essence of Christianity, that the darkness of sin that chains and binds us is broken by the light of the sun—or, the light of the Son, Jesus Christ. Jesus stands in the spaces of emptiness in our hearts and fills us with his love and peace. Eventually, we learn to abide in this love so that we can share the source of this love with others. But sharing this love means respecting others and introducing God in such a way that respects the uniqueness of the individual and their God-given free will. In this, St. Patrick was a master at introducing Christianity to the Irish, and his approach holds many lessons for us.

Patrick did not seek to dominate, convert, or conquer the Irish through force or violence. Instead, he found a way to bless and affirm some of their ancient beliefs and practices by finding a note of harmony with Christianity. For example, the Celts worshipped the sun and so St. Patrick encircled the Roman cross with the sun, which gives us the unique cross of Celtic spirituality: the Celtic cross, which symbolizes the victory of light over the permanent darkness of decay.

St. Patrick also knew that the Celts worshipped their Gods out of a sense of fear: fear of bad weather, poor harvests, and famine. If the gods could be appeased, then they would be happy and life would be harmonious. If the gods were angered, that anger was passed on to the people. Fear was the dominant emotion of the Celts. St. Patrick, by contrast, introduced Christ to the Irish as a God of love, not a God of fear. When Patrick was with the shepherds on the mountains, Christ was portrayed as a shepherd. When Patrick was with the fishermen on the coasts and the lakes of Ireland, Christ was portrayed as a fisherman and St. Patrick emphasized those stories from Jesus' life when he was on the water.

So it is that St. Patrick brought faith learning and faith living together. He listened to their concerns, engaged in dialogue with them, and challenged them from a place of respect, not dominance. As a result of how God was introduced to the Irish, Ireland is unique in having few early Christian martyrs. Who could fear a God that was born as a helpless infant in a stable? Who could fear a God who was a shepherd or a fisherman? Patrick shared with them that Jesus is God's son who came to save all people, the enslaved and the free.

Through the incarnation, Jesus entered our world as one of us and trampled down the darkness of death so that we could share in his life as the light of the world. His light is not fleeting; nor will it diminish, no matter what darkness we find ourselves in. He is there with us because we were created for him. He knows our pain and our shadows but loves us all the more for the light that is within.

In the Gospel of John, chapter 11, verses 1–43, we read of Jesus raising Lazarus from the dead. In various translations of that passage, we read that Jesus loosens the bonds of death that entombed Lazarus. If we examine our own lives, we can identify those patterns of death and destruction that entomb us in a cave of darkness. Often they are patterns of behavior. They are familiar, safe, and easy. These habits, behaviors, or what we call sins cocoon us into a strange hibernation of being. We are neither dead nor alive but exiled from our fellow beings in a self-imposed state of limbo. We become the "lukewarm" people mentioned in the book of Revelation, "neither cold nor hot" (Revelation 3:16). Joy is muted, happiness is fleeting. But there comes a thin time or a thin season, often accompanied by intense suffering, when we must break through the bonds of this entombment, lest we become trapped forever and die. We break through and we break free. Out of the cocoon, as we know, emerges the butterfly: glorious, majestic, and vibrant.

With the fast pace of life these days, the inner voice in the shadow of our hearts is drowned out. We trade authenticity and wholeness for pragmatic and efficient. We feel the "thinness" and growth edges before us, but the frenetic pace of our lives leaves little time for introspection and self-reflection, which are necessary for us to live a full life. Can you remember the last time you sat and reflected upon your life rather than rushing through the day? In our journey through the first part of this book, we've broken down some pretty heavy concepts: our identity, what we stuff in our junk drawers (our fears), and in this chapter, the fears that imprison us and prevent us from moving into the light. In the next part, we will move to *break through* some of these experiences and work toward the process of breaking free.

Your Thin Place: The Darkness

Irish seanfhocal (old word): Is doimhin é poll an
amhrais.
Translation: Deep is the hole of doubt.

Breaking Open

Many times, we are so busy getting through life that we forget what it means to truly live. Doubts and fears can plague us. Rather than moving ahead, we may remain fixated on the negatives and get trapped in the past. But we must develop the ability to be at peace with ourselves and, in doing so, will come to better awareness of who we are and how God's grace is moving through it.

Breaking Through

Light cannot see inside things.
That is what the dark is for:
Minding the interior,
Nurturing the draw of growth
Through places where death
In its own way turns into life.[1]

—John O'Donohue, "For Light"

- What is the great fear that has chained you to the wall? Who are your shadow companions in the cave?
- Which fear is greater, the fear of being chained in the dark or the pain from the light of truth?
- What is the truth that waits for you outside the cave?
- What would it take for you to loosen the bonds of your own entombment?

---

1. *To Bless the Space Between Us: A Book of Blessings* (New York: Doubleday, 2008).

Breaking Free

*The people walking in darkness have seen a great
light; On those living in the land of deep
darkness a light has dawned.*

—Isaiah 9:2

Twilight is that intermediary time between the dark and the light. Often
when we go through painful experiences, all we see is the darkness, and
we fail to see the small slivers of twilight. This week, choose one of the
most difficult times of your life and look for twilight glimmers of hope
that you might have missed before.

Part Two
Crossing the Threshold

*A river cuts through rock, not because
of its power, but because of its
persistence.*

—Jim Watkins

The only way out is through.

—Anonymous

4

Mirror, Mirror

*Irish seanfhocal (old word): Dá fhada an lá
tagann an tráthnóna.
Translation: No matter how long the day, the
evening will come.*

Boy meets girl.

It's an old story. Boy meets girl, girl falls in love with boy, boy rejects girl, girl pines for boy. Life moves on. It might be familiar to us because it's part of our story or the story of someone we know. Unrequited love has been an endless fountain of creative juice for music, movies, myths, and legends. Throughout life, we learn that we are formed by those who love us and those who refuse to love us.

Meet Echo.

Echo fell in love with a boy well known for his good looks. At the ripe old age of sixteen, this boy had left a trail of tears and destruction behind him in the hearts of those he broke. One day Echo secretly follows him into the woods where he was walking. Like so many women before her, she was smitten.

The boy, sensing that someone is following him, turns to ask, "Who's there?" Now, by a strange twist of fate, Echo was not able to dialogue with others, only mimic them. When the boy speaks to her, Echo cannot respond; all she can do is parrot back what was said to her. "Who's there?" he asks. "Who's there?" she repeats to the boy and steps forward to embrace him. The boy cruelly rejects Echo, and Echo is devastated. She withdraws back into the world of silence where the only voice she can dialogue with is the voice inside her head. She withers away until all that is left of her are the words of others. The young boy, wholly unconcerned with Echo or her feelings, swiftly moves on with his life. But one day something in a pool of water catches his eye.

Sitting down, he reaches in to grasp what he sees, but it continues to elude him. He cannot pull himself away from the pool, and little by little, what he sees in the water continues to haunt him until he cannot sleep or eat. Consumed with a fire that burns from the inside out, the boy becomes totally absorbed in himself and drowns, leaving only a reminder of his life in the form of a small white and gold flower. The name of that flower is the narcissus.

This story is of course the ancient tale of Narcissus and Echo, found in Ovid's *Metamorphoses*, and it has a lot to teach us about loving ourselves and others, especially in today's highly selfie-driven culture of social media.

Self-Absorption and Echoing

At the heart of the story of Narcissus and Echo are the themes of self-knowledge and self-love. In his self-absorption, Narcissus is unable to empathize and build lasting relationships with others. Known for his good looks, he uses his appearance to make an initial connection with others but remains unfulfilled forever. What does he see in the pool of water that captivates him? It is an image of perfection that draws him in, an image of himself. Unable to tear himself away, he becomes consumed inside with an ache that no other person can satisfy. His spirit begins to wither but is closely followed by his body, and eventually Narcissus drowns in this reflection. In Ovid's tale, Narcissus disappears, leaving behind only a small pretty flower, but in other versions of the story, Narcissus is driven to commit suicide. This story is where the term *narcissist* comes from. Like Narcissus, narcissists never find it within themselves to love anyone more than they love themselves.

By contrast, Echo is a classic codependent personality, deriving her self-worth from what others give her. She has no voice of her own, only that which comes from echoing others. Spurned from an unrequited love, she too dwindles to nothingness until all that is left is the echo of her voice, reverberating around glens and forests. Narcissus's natural sense of who he is has been corrupted by his extreme focus on himself, while Echo's has been denigrated to nothingness. If Narcissus is self-absorbed, then Echo is other-absorbed.

Both are recipes for disaster.

Scratching the Surface of the Self

Selfishness and selflessness have the same root—*self*—and as such, they are related concepts. When we derive our worth from others, we will become an echo or shadow of who we are called to be. If we are totally self-absorbed, putting only ourselves first, what we see in the mirror will be a distorted and exaggerated image of ourselves and others. If we do not take care of ourselves and avoid the mirror of our own needs, we limit our own possibilities and potential. Total selflessness is as dangerous as complete selfishness because both are extremes. The myth of Narcissus and Echo reminds us that there is a fine line between loving others more than we love ourselves and loving ourselves to the detriment of others. In this story, we also see the danger of being preoccupied with perfection.

At various times when my desire to have a clean house veered toward compulsion, a wise friend reminded me that "the perfect is the enemy of the good." Good enough is good enough. Just a note on the cleaning: having children effectively ended my ability to ever have a totally clean house! The small handprints on the doors, the walls, and the mirrors tell their own story, and one day they won't be there anymore. So, I leave them as they are unless they are particularly gross, and I am content with the reminders of my children's "littleness." Fixation on and obsession with perfection never end well, particularly in our environment today.

Today we exist in a world that puts a premium on self-actualization, self-importance, and perfection. The culture of perfection dominates our time and creates a false world based on appearance and deceit. The old maxim "the Lord helps those who help themselves" is certainly true (although it's not from the Bible), but taken to an extreme, it can lead us, like Narcissus, to become lost in a pool of self-absorption and vanity. Or like Echo, we are attracted to those who will never love us, and we become absorbed in this rejection until our voice disappears and the only words left are the echoes of others' voices and words. Echo found that because she projected all her self-worth on a person who could never reciprocate her love, she could not fully love herself either. Narcissus was incapable of loving anyone more than himself because he was filled with his own self-importance. The more inflated our sense of self-importance, the less room there is for other people and for God. Self-importance and self-esteem are not the same thing. You can have very low self-esteem but an inflated view of your importance. We meet people like this all the time as we navigate life; sometimes we even fall in love with people like Narcissus and Echo. Sometimes we meet these tendencies in ourselves.

The Renaissance philosopher René Descartes's famous pronunciation "I think, therefore I am" has maybe been replaced with "I tweet, therefore I am" or "I show up on a Google search, therefore I exist." We may measure our happiness by the number of followers we have online or the number of likes we get on social media.

It was an actual pool of water that caught Narcissus's eye, but today one of the new pools to mirror our self-absorption is social media, where we see clearly the "echo chamber" effect.

Let's take a look.

We live in the telecommunications era, a revolutionary time that promises a larger but more humanly connected world. A world in which information is instant, clickable, and shareable. A world in which relationships can be built without ever sitting down face-to-face. A world in which families who live apart can draw close to each other through the magic of technology. Now several years into this era, we wonder if the world has become more connected through social media or more disconnected, at least on the human level.

The word *telecommunication* literally means "distant communications." Certainly, as an immigrant, I've received social media as an invaluable tool for connecting with my family in Ireland. It helps ease the loneliness that comes with being apart from them. I can see pictures of my nieces and nephews during the holidays, catch up with my father on Skype, and congratulate and commiserate over the local news. But this is not a substitute for actually being with my family. Social media are tools that help build and maintain relationships. Outside of our immediate family and friends, social media connect us with ever-larger networks of relationships. But according to some researchers, those relationships may be more insular than our in-person interactions.

According to research from *Cyberpsychology: Journal of Pyschosocial Research on Cyperspace*, people tend to look for news and information that confirm what they already believe. This is known as confirmation bias. When there is breaking news, it spreads like wildfire on social media and creates what is known as an "echo chamber."[2]

This echo chamber creates a space in which we receive information that echoes, or confirms, like-minded opinions and thoughts from others with whom we agree. This creates a network of similarly minded people with shared values who accept their preferred sources as truth and continue to share and perpetuate preferred information, whether or not it is true, partially accurate, or skewed toward a specific agenda. This leads to a proliferation of biased narratives fueled by unsubstantiated rumors and mistrust. Similarly minded can often mean singularly minded, because those who we don't agree with are silenced, ignored, and marginalized. We can "hide" people on social media who irritate us and, in doing so, marginalize their voices, an option we don't have when we are face-to-face. Like Narcissus, we see only what we want to see and, similar to Echo, the voice of "the other" replaces our own voice.

Echo chambers similarly exist in our spiritual lives.

"But Jesus said to love one another as I have loved you!" said Mary, exasperated, to the women gathered at our weekly Bible study. Sitting in the church basement, our women's group was in the midst of a very heated discussion about the Beatitudes and how to care for the poor. "We have to love those who are marginalized, especially the poor and the homeless, and find ways to reach out!" Mary passionately stated.

"But Jesus also told us that he came to fulfill the spirit of the law," Veronica piped up. "So, if those who are poor break the law, do they deserve our care and support? The Lord helps those who help themselves, right?"

I was stunned. Mary left the room, and the conversation turned to a "safer" Beatitude like "blessed are the meek."

Jesus wept.

---

2. Luzsa, R., & Mayr, (2021). False consensus in the echo chamber: Exposure to favorably biased social media news feeds leads to increased perception of public support for own opinions. *Cyberpsychology: Journal of Psychosocial Research on Cyberspace, 15*(1), Article 3. https://doi.org/10.5817/CP2021-1-3.

Spiritual echo chambers characterize many discussions today about Christianity and religion, which become polarizing and mistrustful instead of open and dialogical. We project negative thoughts about "the other" and become focused on serving those inside our own circle. Uncomfortable with the demands of the Gospel, we may choose which parts of the Gospel we want to focus on and ignore the rest. We distort what we perceive as valuable and change it to fit our own narrative, or we generalize large swaths of the message of the Gospel and ignore nuances and other perspectives. Research into neurolinguistic programming (NLP) reveals that human beings generally filter out information in three ways: we delete it, distort it (omitting information or adjusting the narrative to fit our own preferences), or generalize it.

Christianity is a big tent in which saints and sinners walk together, where ragtag fishermen and courageous women sat at the feet of Jesus yearning for truth, for greater understanding of the God who created them and the world around them. Such a community is damaged by the distortion and judgment that happen within a spiritual echo chamber.

Spiritual echo chambers are dangerous because we become self-referential and closed instead of open and thoughtful. Our conversations use insider language, jargon that people outside the group don't understand. Young people might, for example, write us off as irrelevant and out of touch. When we "preach to the choir," we become comfortable and mollified instead of invigorated and stirred up. When we reduce conversations about faith to a caste system or an ideology, we miss the heart of the Gospel: following Jesus Christ and his teachings so as to be transformed in mind, body, and spirit, not just individually but collectively.

What we narrowly talk about in closed circles isn't going to change the world without thoughtful action. We must get out of our spiritual echo chambers and engage in a dialogue with others who do not live like us, think like us, love like us, pray like us, or act like us.

Clearly, this has implications for how we relate to one another. Sitting down with family members and having conversations exposes us to a broad range of opinions and thoughts about issues that are necessary for us to grow and develop. Hearing from someone in person, taking the time to question them and, most important, listen to them, helps us become more empathetic, more compassionate, and more thoughtful. We are challenged, and when we are challenged, we grow. We can listen for cues where we can fill gaps in understanding with information. We find ways to connect our story to their story, finding common ground, and to move out of our pool of self-absorption. Just as you cannot read a book when it is an inch from your face, you will be unable to reflect upon your life if you are an inch from the pool or the mirror.

That's why the healthiest thing that you can do is to break through the mirror of your self-importance to see yourself as you truly are.

Breaking the Mirror

How you experience life depends a lot on your perspective.

Breaking the mirror of self-importance, pride, and—yes—even our narcissistic tendencies is tough stuff, but we have to do it if we want to live a truly joyful life. Don't misunderstand me: there's nothing wrong with building ourselves up or putting ourselves first once in a while. But, as I mentioned earlier, self-esteem and self-importance are not the same thing. Self-importance places our demands above the needs of others without regard to their intrinsic value and dignity. Narcissists see people as a means to an end and will end up unfulfilled and dissatisfied forever. Nothing or no one is ever good enough. Idealism gives way to a fruitless striving for perfection. Narcissus was never able to scratch the surface of who he was created to be, and he remained content with his reflection in the search for who he was. If only some-one had told him to "look a little deeper," he might have realized that staying at the surface was killing him. If only he had the courage to break the mirror of self-importance!

Like Narcissus, we can stay at the surface all our lives, or we can look a little deeper to see what the eye doesn't always see. There needs to be a balance between the temporal (what is often in Ireland called the "here and now") and the eternal (the "not-yet"), the ancient and new, the known and the unknown, and the exterior and the interior, for our lives to be balanced. Focusing on our exterior life to excess will always come at the expense of our interiority.

After breaking up with my high school boyfriend of six years, which I dealt with by partying way too hard in college, I arrived in Wisconsin nursing a bruised heart and a crushed spirit. My faith was shaky and my sense of self-worth even shakier. The cumulative effects of trauma and woundedness pushed me to places where I hurt myself and others. "Too much" sums up this part of my life: I partied too much, drank too much, and ate too much. Entering a thin place? I couldn't have cared less. I sat chained in my cave and didn't want to turn to the light. But one day I took a hard look in the mirror and saw myself as if for the first time. I didn't like what I saw.

But instead of doing the inner work that was needed, I threw myself into my appearance and began to work out excessively. My inner voice told me that I couldn't control the past or the future, but I believed that I could control how I looked and so began to compet-itively body build. Very quickly, bodybuilding and calorie counting took over my life. One day my mother called me after I had sent her some new pictures of myself. "How long did you spend in the gym this week?" she asked. Mentally I did the math. "Twenty-one hours," I told her. "How many hours did you spend nourishing your soul or doing anything to get to the bottom of what's going on in your life, Julianne?" she asked.

Ouch. My mother was never one to mince words.

I hung up the phone, annoyed with her, but deep down I knew she was right. Physically I was in the best shape of my life, but mentally and spiritually I was a mess. At night, I walked in the quiet, sometimes for two hours at a time, processing the pain that was seething deep down in my soul. "There's a name for this," my friend Mike said. "What is it?" I asked him. "Soul sickness," he answered. "And there ain't no hospital that you can go to for that one."

There isn't a medical hospital for soul sickness, but there is a spiritual hospital. One day I walked into a small country church and sat down in the peace and quiet. With the scent of incense in the air, I held up the pieces of my life to God and talked to him from my heart. The searing pangs of anguish in my soul bubbled up, and I poured out my pain and unhappiness. Piece by piece, the carefully crafted mirror of my self-absorption began to crack, and eventually it shattered. I was in the most sacred "thinnest space" I had ever walked into, and God shined a light in the darkness. With time and a good counselor on my side, I stopped working out and instead focused on walking and eating for pleasure, not expediency. I spent more time in prayer, read Scripture, and began to like what I saw reflected in the mirror of my life.

The mirror that we hold up to ourselves, especially the one that we often project on social media, is not the true reflection of who we are created to be. It is our spiritual echo chamber. In the Pinterest perfection of our self-selected imagery, many of us are crying out to be loved as we really are—not for what we do, what we look like, how much we weigh, or who we are dating, but for who we really are.

Self-esteem is related to our sense of self-worth and value as a human being. If you have a sense of your own innate dignity and value, you begin to understand that your self-worth does not come from other creatures but from the One who created you. The question that is longing for a voice as we look in the mirror is often this one: "If God knew who I really was, would he still love me anyway?" The answer is yes. He knows, he sees, and he accepts and loves you, flaws and all. Like a watermark on paper that is invisible to the eye until held to the light, your self-worth increases as you grow closer to the true source of light, which is God. You are worthy because you have been created by God.

As a reflection of God, we have worth and value far beyond anything this world has to offer. So go ahead and smash the glass on what others think of you; it doesn't matter in the end anyway. Break through the bonds of what others think and move deeply into breaking through to the person you were always meant to be. As we say in Ireland, "It will stand to you" (meaning "it will benefit you"), especially as you break through some difficult times, or what the Irish call "the thin times."

Your Thin Place: Mirror, Mirror

*Irish seanfhocal (old word): Dá fhada an lá
tagann an tráthnóna.
Translation: No matter how long the day, the
evening will come.*

Breaking Open

This *seanfhocal* doesn't always translate as well as some other proverbs because the Celts viewed time as an unbroken circle, much like the love of God. We typically view the morning as the beginning of the day, and the end of the day, as nightfall. For the Celts, however, night was the beginning of the day. Nonetheless, the meaning behind this lovely expression is that no matter what happens to you on a particularly bad day, a new day is dawning before you, and with it, new experiences. Darkness gives way to the light, and light gives way to the dark.

Breaking Through

- Choose three words that reflect who you are. What do you want to reflect to the world?
- Have you ever had a "shatter the mirror" experience? What happened? How did others react? Have you ever been subjected to public shaming? What was the most harrowing aspect of that experience? Did new life come from this experience?
- What does your spiritual echo chamber look like?

Breaking Free

*I praise you because I am fearfully and
wonderfully made; your works are wonderful, I
know that full well.*

—Psalm 139:14

This week, be alert for opportunities to break through your spiritual echo chamber. Resist the tendency to confirm your own ideas and thoughts and instead strive to be open and flexible. Spend time thanking God for the diversity of the world and the new relationships, opportunities, and events that are around every corner.

5

The Thin Times

Irish seanfhocal (old word): Ní fhaghann cos' na comhnaidh aon nídh.
Translation: The foot at rest meets nothing.

"I think I'm going to get Botox," my mother told me emotionally one day over the phone. "Whaaat?" I responded. "Mammy, why would you do that?" I asked her, confused. "I look old," she said. "I'm tired." At this time, my mother had not even turned fifty, but I could hear the weariness in her voice. "I'm coming home," I told her. "Give me a few weeks to book my flight, don't do anything before then, and let's talk about this." She agreed. Deep down in my heart, I knew my mother well enough to know that her desire to get Botox was not actually about Botox at all. It was a symptom of something much, much deeper.

Freeze-Frame, Freeze Pain

Sitting in my mother's sunny yellow kitchen a couple of weeks later, I could see for myself just how exhausted she was. It was a deep-down tired that cut to her very soul: spiritual exhaustion. "What's going on?" I asked. It was a rare day that day, for she opened up to me and talked for hours. Pouring out a tsunami of pain, she shared how the death of her mother and her sister had affected her, along with some difficult experiences, including the pain of multiple miscarriages. "That's why I want to get Botox" she said. "I want to see a different face when I look in the mirror." I reached out to take her hand. My mother was not a "touchy-feely" person, but that day she sat silently as I held her hand.

When we go through any kind of intense pain, a transformation is waiting to take place. We wear that pain and that transformation on our hearts and our faces. The Irish poet and philosopher John O'Donohue throughout his writings frequently calls our faces the "icon of creation." Our faces are the map of our souls in our journey through life. Pain, grief, sadness, joy, relief, and bitterness all wash over the contours of our face, and as we change, our faces change with us. The contours of our face change not just with the seasons but with our response to pain and joy. A wonderful example of this is my husband's grandmother Anna.

A proud Polish woman, Anna lived to be ninety-eight years old, and her face told its own story of love and loss, restlessness and peace. It was a puzzle to me, though, because one side of her face was noticeably more wrinkled than the other side. I learned why when we went one day to pray. Anna generally had the same routine each day and loved to pray the rosary while sitting in the sunshine on her dock by the lake or on her porch. She wore no sunscreen and so the sun beamed its illuminate rays more directly on one side of her face; the other was shaded. As the years progressed, the side that was always turned to the sun was more wrinkled than the other side. When I pointed this out to her, she laughed. "I wouldn't take back a single wrinkle," she said, "for all the peace that came with those prayers."

Our faces change as we change. We may not stop to think of it often, but our mind, body, and spirit all respond to life in their own way, consciously and unconsciously. As we grow older, we become more aware of time etching and contouring our faces a little at a time. Not just with age or time, but also with circumstances. Just as a smile can light up a face, grief can do remarkable things as it etches its way across the features. I heard many stories in Ireland of those whose hair literally turned "white overnight" with the weight of grief and loss after a tragic death.

But the way that we live also affects the face that the world sees.

Your Face Is the Threshold of Your Inner World

Jean-Paul Sartre, the noted existentialist philosopher, wrote that we are born with a face that is largely the result of genetics, but after a time, how we live and what we believe will show on our faces. We cannot totally escape the past because the imprint of our ancestors reveals the character of our face. We may have our grandmother's eye color or our father's nose. We might have our mother's heart-shaped face or our father's strong nose. However, Sartre claims that, eventually, other factors in life will begin to influence our faces. What we hold inside of us will eventually seep out to the surface, no matter how hard we try to keep it hidden. For example, if life has made you a bitter, mean-spirited, and angry person, it will be incredibly difficult to keep those thoughts from your face. Similarly, if you are joyful and have a contagious effervescence for life, your face will show that same energy. At some point in our lives, our genetics will be superseded by our environment and the choices we make. To put it another way, what you believe on the inside will eventually show on the outside, especially on your face. Your interior life will manifest on the exterior.

In time, the wrinkles and lines that you develop become appropriate to your character and your experiences. Think, for example, of Mother Teresa's face: lined and wrinkled but also filled with peace. Or the face of the Dalai Lama: noble and strong. But if you think of the faces of celebrities or even family members whose lives have been ravaged by the scourge of addiction, their face tells a different story. The opioid crisis in particular has changed the face of drug use from being an underground subculture to a problem that affects all walks of life. The derogatory terms *meth heads* or *meth face* speak to a reality of just how much drug use changes the faces of our loved ones.

Eventually our faces mirror our thoughts, beliefs, practices, and experiences. Despite the fact that some people are very good at projecting what is often called a "poker face," we can never hide from the world who we truly are, for our faces are always visible to others.

Our face is the threshold of our own inner world, and we become its gatekeeper. Thresholds were important to the Celts, who were drawn to the edges and margins of life. Thresholds mark the space between the inner and the outer, the interior and the exterior. To this day, the rustic stone walls of the west of Ireland mark spaces and boundaries as thresholds between properties of different landowners. Darkness and light are marked by their own fluid thresholds of twilight and dawn. In the dim light, shadows are cast, and we find rest and solace, as the Scriptures tell us: "Stand at the crossroads, and look, and ask for the ancient paths, where the good way lies; and walk in it, and find rest for your souls" (Jeremiah 6:16). In rural parts of Ireland, you might still find some of the old "half-doors" that mediate the space between inside and outside by allowing the homeowner to open the door fully or partway.

We can do the same with our face. We can project open or closed, apathetic or joyful, and inviting or indifferent. Depending on what we want to hide, our face becomes something not to *face* the world but instead a mask used to hide our pain. We often aren't even aware of this mask until we look into the mirror one day and don't recognize the person looking back at us. Confronting what we see and who we are takes courage. The body protects itself, and pain often forces us to adopt a mask of pretension out of self-preservation.

My mother wanted to hide her pain and so instead of doing the difficult work of looking within, she looked to a solution provided by the outside world to freeze her face. Her solution was Botox! A bit drastic but it made sense to my mother. After we talked about the source of her sadness, she came to realize that freezing her face might have made her temporarily happy, but it was unlikely to freeze her pain.

Just in case you think that I am super uptight about personal enhancement, let me assure you that I'm not. There's nothing wrong with enhancing what has been given naturally to us as long as we keep things in perspective. But Botox injections wouldn't have solved the pain in my mother's soul any more than pain is healed by smoothing over its wrinkles. Her pain was born of grief, and the only way through that grief was to deal with its source. "The only way out is through," as the popular expression goes. My mother found that the best way to cope with her pain was to talk it out and also to walk it out, which she did literally by joining a mountain walking group. Afterward we would talk about her experiences, and I would refer to this time in my mother's life as "pilgrimaging through her pain."

Walking It Out: The Pilgrimage of Pain

As noted earlier, pilgrimage has been important to the Irish as a way of walking out our need for forgiveness, to express repentance, to give thanks, or for the myriad other reasons that people undertake pilgrimage. Pilgrimage is a spiritual catalyst for transformation. In contrast with a trip where we visit a specific place as a guest or as a visitor, pilgrimages are times when you journey inward even if your body is facing outward. As your outward body moves, inside, the real work is happening.

Before she climbed Ireland's highest mountain, Carrauntoohil, my mother called and said, "You know, it would be a lot easier if I could take something for the grief." "What do you mean?" I asked her. "Oh, you know, like a pill or a tablet," she said. We both laughed but also acknowledged the pain of what lay ahead in facing her grief. "We all know," I responded, "that life would be so much duller if all we knew was happiness and never pain." "Hard to argue with that one," she said. Then she set out to begin the slow trek through her memories and the choices she had made.

Carrauntoohil is a difficult climb, with the weather in the west of Ireland being notoriously fickle. There are pictures of my mother at each stage of the journey: at the bottom of the climb, making her way up the mountain, at the top of the mountain, and again when she came down. What is so fascinating to me is how much her face changed through these pilgrimages. Starting out tense and weary, she ended her journey exhilarated and lighter, even when she was pushing the edge of her physical limits.

What my mother found is not new. Grief, loss, and pain cut to the heart, and there's nothing you can take in pill form when your soul is sick. While we have hospitals that treat physical, emotional, and mental health, when it comes to "soul sickness" there isn't a special hospital that can rehabilitate us in the same way. There isn't a human experience that can kiss the boo-boo away as I do with my children. Spiritual boo-boos require their own kind of medicine to treat the causes at the root, down to the core. Fortunately, we don't have to go it alone.

My mother invited Jesus, the Soul Healer, the Divine Physician, into the space in her soul that was weary and exhausted. She never regretted it. Even as she lay dying from cancer four days after her fifty-fourth birthday, she would repeat her own little mantra to make it through the pain. "May the precious blood of Christ flow through me today, thank you, Jesus," she would whisper. It was her greatest prayer and the one that took her home to her eternal rest, finally at peace with who she was and where God was calling her to be.

As I discovered, especially in losing my mother, there is no medicine you can take for grief. There is no pill that magically makes it all better, and despite what the world tells us, life isn't about the absence of pain and suffering but about our ability to live with it, to cope with it, and to move with it.

Pain is a threshold of growth. If we miss the pain, then we also miss the growth in the slow work of transformation that is happening, often unnoticed. What the eye doesn't see, as the popular saying goes, the heart won't grieve over.

Out of sight, however, does not mean out of soul. The people we love walk with us every day, and they are especially close to us in the memory of special places and events. My mother found great comfort in these "thin places" that are scattered around Ireland, as numerous as the stars in the sky. Let's continue to take a look at these "thin places" in our lives.

Thin Spaces and Places

Growing up in Ireland, I had a sense of mystery and spirituality permeating daily life, even if the understanding of Ireland as the land of "saints and scholars" has waned. The misty weather, the ruins that are scattered throughout the country, and the lingering superstitions that are a part of the tapestry of Irish culture—all contribute to a sense of mystery that settles into your bones. While mystery is largely associated today with magic and superstition, thin places are spaces of mystery and encounter—where we meet God, in ourselves and in others. They are places imbued with a sense of ancient longing, where we can feel and discern the naked truth of life, not just with our five senses but also with our sixth. This is seen especially in the respect the Irish have for spirits and the places where the spirit folk gather such as fairy forts or fairy trees.

Ring forts were built around the Bronze Age up until 1000 BC. Today they are essentially the remains of ancient circular fortifications, but most people in Ireland know them as fairy forts and generally avoid disturbing them. The Irish generally believed it was unlucky to call fairies by the name "fairy" and referred to them in Gaelic in the following ways:

Na daoine maithe (the good people)
Na daoine uaisle (the gentry)
Bunadh na gcnoc (the people of the hills)

Children are warned to avoid the places where fairies gather, such as ring forts. Farmers will plow their fields around these forts, and roads have been diverted to preserve them as sacred spaces. Certain trees are also associated with the "other world," and great care is taken with respect to them. For example, when I was growing up, I was never allowed to play near hawthorn or whitethorn trees because they are trees that are associated with "the little people" and those who walk before us in the form of spirits.

For the Irish, surrounded by the ruins of ancient castles and monastic villages, the wisdom of those who have passed on from our communities and families is just a whisper away. Every day as I went to secondary school (the Irish equivalent of middle and high school), I passed megalithic tombs known as portal tombs (or dolmens), ring forts or "fairy forts" where puca (spirits) gather, and the ruins of manors and castles, some recent and others from a thousand years ago.

Embedded in Celtic beliefs and practices is the understanding that there is more to the world than we can see, and the burial tombs and graveyards of Ireland are a constant reminder that the old and the new can live side by side in harmony. Fairy forts, tombs, and dolmens are places where conversation between the known and the unknown continues to take place as people continue to gather at these sacred places. We live in a world that is both hidden and revealed, seen and unseen, mysterious and yet known.

Even today, when the practice of Catholicism is declining in Ireland, people still gather at these ancient places to search for meaning in their lives, particularly at sites called "holy wells." Surveys conducted in Ireland estimate that there are perhaps 2,500–3,000 holy wells in Ireland. Some of them are so famous that they can be found on ordinance survey maps, some are known only to locals by word of mouth, and many have been lost to the annals of history. A good number of the wells are associated with various saints of Ireland, but their origins predate Christianity by thousands of years. Holy wells are usually spring fed and are circular or oval. They may be situated by a lone tree, often an oak, for oak trees were sacred to the Celts, or they may be located in the copse of a nondescript field. The Irish consider holy wells to be thin places that radiate a sense of otherworldliness, places where people of all ages and faiths still gather to mourn, to pray, to remember, and to celebrate. Many people today approach holy wells with the same sense of reverence that they have done in the past. They will often take their shoes off and walk barefoot around the well or dip their feet and hands into it. I took a group of pilgrims to a special holy well in Ireland some years ago, and we sat and watched a steady trickle of people, the young and the old, the devout and the searching, all gather in this thin place.

Cloaked in history, these ancient ruins seep into the imagination, encouraging us to see "beyond the beyond." Thin places are not just "over there" in Ireland but also "in here"—in our mind, in our heart, and in our soul. We are drawn to these thin places such as holy wells that encourage us to look at our own thin places, with all their light and shadow, as places of healing. Your own "healing well" might be in your garden or a seat in your favorite chair by a window. We do not have to learn how to speak to God in these thin places, for God is already present to us. This encourages us to see the sacramental nature of life—that all of life has been made sacred because it was created by a God at the heart of life rather than distant and away from life.

This recovery of the shadow aspect of life, the place where mystery dwells, is, I believe, the place where faith and religious imagination dwell, and it is the playground of God in our hearts. It is the place where we feel delight, true joy, and an abiding sense of peace. Threshold or liminal places take us from one place to another, in our surroundings but also inside of ourselves. Just as the half-doors of Ireland can open in and out at the same time, our eyes navigate this inside-outside dynamic for our lives. Our eyes become a gatekeeper for what we absorb and what we reject, and yet we rarely are discerning in terms of the visual pollution that surrounds us. If beauty is in the eye of the beholder, so too is prejudice and avarice. What we see often becomes what we believe, and what we believe often becomes how we live. Let's take a deeper look at this concept.

In the Eye of the Beholder

Our eyes are intensely powerful. They are physical portals that mediate messages to our brains and process information. When we look at something repeatedly, it becomes a part of our being, and if we are unguarded, it can seep into our consciousness. "What you put your mind to often grows," my mother used to say, which is a nod to the Irish expression *An rud a lionas an tsuil lionann se an croi*, which means "What fills the eye, fills the heart." My love for collecting sea glass has taught me that our eyes have the ability to magnify what we see in a positive and negative sense when it comes to what our eye accepts or rejects. A friend of mine who has lived by the water for many years once remarked, "It must be the luck of the Irish that you find beach glass all the time because I have lived here for twenty years and have never found anything!" I assured her that finding beach glass has less to do with luck and more to do with being aware of the properties of the glass and knowing where to look. Just because we do not see beach glass does not mean that it is not there. We took a walk together, and I explained to her a few things that I had learned through the years, such as the best time of the day to search for glass, the places where it washes up, and even how to walk so that it can be spotted more easily. After we walked for ten minutes or so, lo and behold, she found her first piece of glass!

When we collect certain items, our eye naturally picks out what it is that we look for. For example, if you collect elephant figures, in a store you will find one easily enough. I do not collect elephant figures, so if I went into the same store, it is unlikely that my eyes would spot the figure, since I am not looking for it. My focus would not be attuned for a particular item and so would skip over it. When our eyes "weed out" information, we lose perspective. We do this to others, but we also exercise the same critical eye when it comes to ourselves.

We can become desensitized and numb to violence depicted on television. Young people are particularly vulnerable to the effects of toxic imagery and pornography, especially on social media. We are constantly bombarded with advertisements enticing us to become better, skinnier, wealthier, and less wrinkly versions of ourselves and, over time, we tune out. Noise is not simply about sound but also visual disturbance and can affect us deeply. Social media can increase anxiety as we see others who apparently have more than us even though we know that what we are seeing is not always true.

Our eyes "see" but do not always perceive. This can also be true of our relationship with God. St. Ignatius of Loyola urged his followers to find God "in all things," and if we seek to find God in our daily lives, God will speak to us, but first we must attune our presence to him. God speaks, often in the silence of our hearts, but we are often so busy and distracted that we fail to see him. Jesus says to us "seek and you will find" (Luke 11:9), and yet how often do we fail to seek Jesus and see his face in our lives? Tune out the visual noise. Consciously attune your eye toward the good, in yourself and others, by looking for beauty.

If we look upon the world with the eyes of wisdom and faith, beauty and goodness surround us. If we look with the eyes of anger, we will see anger reflected, not just in the people but even in the landscape. Rain will be perceived as harsh and driving instead of nourishing and energetic. The landscape speaks its own language and can be interpreted by people who reflect and listen. Every landscape tells a story of the people who have shaped it, coaxed it into submission, or abandoned it to the elements. Many people gloss over the landscape without thinking, and yet the earth enfolds us and whispers to us its own story. I took a group to Ireland some years ago and watched a wise mystic, David, interpret the landscape masterfully, pointing out nuances that most people missed: the curve of the landscape, the abandoned roads, the sacred ruins buried underneath mounds of earth, and the stories of the people who walked the earth. "If you know where to look, you will know what to look for," David reminded me. In a single generation, the language of the landscape can be lost as we lose the connection to the memory of the earth. The earth keeps its own memories, and so do we.

Our eye often skips over nuances, but if we are careful, we can be surprised by beauty in the most unlikely places. The harsh rawness of the Burren landscape, for example, in the west of Ireland is beautiful for its bleakness and the gray canvas it presents to the eye. But if you look carefully between the cracks or "grikes" that run across its uneven surface, you will see the most beautiful and delicate flora. I grew up in the Wicklow Mountains, and from afar, they can present a flat picture of subtle shades of gray or green. But if you walk into the mountains, you will be surprised by the riot of a heather bloom or the prickliness of the *sceach* or thornbushes that grow willy-nilly. Nestled among gorse and moss are the wild bilberries I used to gather with my mother as a child; these are known as *fraughan*, from the Irish *fraochán*, which are traditionally gathered on the last Sunday in July, known as Fraughan Sunday. The same was true living in Wisconsin, where I used to dread the frozen-tundra winters, with their bleak sky in muted shades of gray and blue until I looked more closely and saw dazzling layers between them.

Be where your feet are, and you will see differently. The same is often true of our spiritual lives. We can experience a winter in our heart even though it may be summer outside. Through difficult times, we experience winters of scarcity and pain. One of the ways that you can tell if you are in a winter season is if you can discern color and vibrancy. In winter it is very hard to see the color in the world. Everything seems to look gray or white. Green is gone, vibrant blue seems banished, and golden light has disappeared. When we go through a winter, it's hard for us to see any color or joy in the world. And yet it is there—we just need to look harder.

In a thin space, if you attune your eye to what is in front of you, you will begin to pick up subtleties in color and variation, your eye will move from the general to the particular, and in death you will see new life. This is especially true in the beauty that lies inside us as we go through our own thin moments.

Embracing Thin Moments

Thin moments, like intense joy, grief, love, pain, heartache, and heartbreak, have the ability to change even how we see life and one another. In the winter of my grief when I lost my mother, all was muted: color, sound, and emotion. Time was measured BTL (before the loss) and ATL (after the loss). My eyes could see beauty, but this did not reach into my grief. I remember one suffocating summer when the weight of the grief felt crushing and it hurt to take a full breath. And then one day, I was driving to work months after my mother had passed away and noticed, it seemed for the first time in forever, how blue the sky was. Beauty pierces pain. It reminds us who we are and invites us to reconnect with our soul.

Beauty is everywhere and in every person. The phrase "wandering eye" doesn't have to have negative connotations: allow your eye to wander over the landscape to appreciate its beauty. God's eye is a wandering eye. God's eye sees you as part of a conversation with the landscape in which you interact. God beholds you in your beauty even when you feel you look ugly on the inside or the outside. If you look with God's eyes upon the world, beauty abounds.

You are beautiful.

Let's not miss beauty because of pain. Let's not miss the beauty that lies at the heart of ourselves even if embracing it is painful.

One of the best gifts you can give someone is to see them, really see them, and to allow yourself to be seen. The real you, the broken-down you and the broken-through you. Break through what your eye sees but does not perceive, what you know but do not understand, and the kaleidoscope of color that's all around you will appear. In breaking through the noise, you become a better listener in that you can perceive what is unspoken. Spirit connects our senses. You hear better because you can see differently.

Don't fix your eye on one flaw you perceive in yourself, one slight from another, or one moment that was hurtful. Break that mirror! Don't allow one moment or one season of thinness to define you without "grabbing a hold of it," as we say in Ireland. Break through that season! Remember the old maxim: boats don't sink because of all the water that is outside of them; they sink because they let the water get inside them. Don't allow others to drill holes in your boat! There are plenty who will do it. Instead, keep on rowing, for life is to be embraced not endured, no matter what we go through. One of the best ways to break through thin moments is with prayer. So let's take a look at that in our next chapter.

Your Thin Place: The Thin Times

Breaking Open

Irish seanfhocal (old word): Ní fhaghann cos' na
comhnaidh aon nídh.
Translation: The foot at rest meets nothing.

This *seanfhocal* reminds us that there is a time for thinking and a time for doing. Often what links the two is the motivation to want to move forward. The same is true of faith. Every step you take brings you closer and deeper into the thin places in your life.

Breaking Through

- Try to identify a "thin place" in your life where you feel God is most present to you. Describe the feeling of being in this place.

- What are some thin moments from your life? How do you feel God's presence reaching into these moments?

- As you think about thin moments, which ones have shaped how you see yourself? As you look at your face, what experiences are etched there?

- What do you see when you look into your eyes?

Breaking Free

The eye is the lamp of the body. If your eyes are
healthy, your whole body will be full of light.

—Matthew 6:22

We all look at our faces at some point during the day, usually when we are washing our face or brushing our teeth. The next time you are in front of the mirror, take a pause. Look at your face and think of how it has changed with time and experience. Now imagine looking at your face through God's eyes. What is the difference?

6

A Pause for Prayer

Irish seanfhocal (old word): Is giorra cabhair Dé
ná an doras.
Translation: God's help is nearer than
the door.

So many of us struggle to know how to pray. And there is no shortage of recommended methods of prayer—it can seem to be quite complicated and elusive. However, I was gifted with a very close and living example of down-to-earth prayer.

Finding Your Prayer Rhythm

From my grandmother Hannah, who we called Nanny, I observed and learned the rhythm of prayer and the power that prayer holds to ground and shape our lives through joy and struggle. Like the days of the ancient Celts, Nanny's day was permeated with prayers—in particular, blessings, that uniquely Celtic form of prayer that grounds even our mundane practices in gratitude. Every act she undertook, from making the bed to baking her soda bread, was grounded in the prayers she murmured under her breath.

Despite having outlived two husbands and raising a small army of children, Nanny welcomed with love, and she had a word of encouragement for the weary, the difficult, and the lost. At her table, she offered her mouthwateringly delicious soda bread and a cup of tea so strong that you could "stand up in it" and dispensed spiritual snippets and practical advice from her chair by her old Aga stove, which she fed generously and regularly with wood and coal.

Nanny was a daily Mass-goer and always sat on the left-hand side of the church in the first or second pew. She was the sacristan and bell ringer of St. Brigid's Church for many years, and despite being a committed Catholic, she wore her faith lightly. By this I mean that she always spoke out of love rather than judgment even when challenging us. She led with her humanity, which was underpinned by her faith. One of the most important conversations we shared was around negativity and avoiding what we call in Ireland "begrudgers." These are people who, no matter what success comes to others, will find a way to begrudge them that success through negativity and withholding. "Alannah," she said to me one day (she called a lot of her grandchildren Alannah, which is the English derivative of *mo leanbh* in Gaelic, which translates to "my child"), "it's far better to say yes to what you love than to say no to what you don't." "What do you mean?" I asked. "Far too many people," she explained, "live with the word *no* etched on their hearts and on their lips rather than living with their *yes* in mind."

This is an important lesson for all of us. How often do we say no to ourselves, to people who are different, to what seems foreign or strange, instead of leading with our yes? In our thoughts, words, and actions we often jump to what we say no to instead of affirming what we hold in common. Living this way, Nanny reminded me, means saying yes to the good you do see, and eventually you will learn to become a more compassionate and understanding person. Affirming the goodness of God's creation in every living thing was a central belief of the Celts, and this understanding also applies to ourselves. Very often, we are harder on ourselves than we are on others, and we reserve the harshest critique for what we say or what we do ourselves.

Each day Nanny retired after lunch to take what she told me was her "Nanny nap." One day, I had reason to disturb her from her nap, and walking into her bedroom, I found her tucked into her bed with a statue of Jesus and Mary under her arm. I burst out laughing! "Don't be making little of Joseph and Mary," she scolded, "for they don't make little of you." And with that, she settled back under the blankets to resume praying the rosary and taking her nap.

Jesus, Mary, and the saints were as real to my grandmother as the people around her. She spoke to our ancestors in her prayers and mentioned them often as being in the company of the saints in her conversations. Nanny's faith was what I call a "living faith"—a faith that flexed with the times as she considered new social problems that were a feature of a modern Ireland described as the Celtic tiger. She considered problems such as the epidemic of drug use or increasing suicide rates through the lens of tradition and her love for the Sacred Heart of Jesus and the Immaculate Heart of Mary. She passed to her eternal home on Mother's Day, which was fitting for a woman who had been a mother to so many. We had prayer cards printed after her funeral with the words by which she lived: "You have gone no further from us than to God and God is very near." *From Nanny I learned that the true rhythm of prayer is found, not in the doing, but in the being, and it is in the being that God is very near.*

For a long time, I thought that praying was something to do. But the heart of prayer is simply being and resting in God. Prayer creates a space for grace in your life. Prayer allows us to slow down and set aside all those distractions that the world is throwing at us so that we can embrace and absorb those special graces from God. Grace is a bestowed-upon, unmerited gift or favor from God; we do not have to earn this gift for God gives us his graces freely. These graces increase as our love and devotion for him increase, especially during times of struggle. God is especially close to us during these times, and I learned just how close when my father was seriously injured in a terrible accident.

The Breastplate of Prayer

It was the summer of my fourteenth birthday. A violent explosion occurred in my father's garage, which was right beside our home. My younger brother Ian and my father's employee Harry witnessed Dad completely engulfed in flames, the melting fibers of his clothing fusing to his body. Harry drove on twisted rural roads to the hospital in Dublin, over an hour away. My father would spend more than six months in a burn unit recovering. The explosion had taken his sight temporarily, and he endured first-, second-, and third-degree burns to 60 percent of his body. We were told to prepare for the worst, but my father stubbornly clung to life. Despite our pleas to see him, Mam refused to take us to see Dad. As the oldest child, even I couldn't understand why. But after a couple of weeks of persistent nagging, she broke down and agreed that we could see Dad. On my fourteenth birthday Mam took my two brothers, my sister, and I to the burn unit of St. James's Hospital in Dublin, where they were keeping Dad, who had been moved out of intensive care.

Dressed in our best, we walked into the public ward in the burn unit where Dad was recovering. To this day, I can smell the strong antiseptic that masked the odor of burnt skin and hair covered over by sterile bandages. We walked into a large room past several men who were unrecognizable in their mummy-like shrouds of bandages and gauze. My mother whispered to us to look away from those who were in their beds, "to preserve their dignity," but curiosity got the better of us. We saw the burnt ends of noses peeking out from bandages, men who had lost fingers, others who were laid on their stomachs since their backs were so badly burned. Time slowed and our feet seemed leaden as we inched our way across the room.

My mother looked around at the narrow beds with a puzzled expression on her face, clearly looking for Dad. "Where is he?" we asked. "They must have moved him" she said, and with that turned us round to face the door. The next moment is one that I will never forget for as long as I live.

As we were walking away, a voice I barely recognized said, "Angie, it's me, I'm here. Don't you recognize me?"

It was my father. So bloated and swollen from the burns that covered his body that he was unrecognizable even to his own family. His throat had been burned raw so not even his voice was recognizable. My mother's face turned gray, and she rushed us into the waiting room and told us to sit still until she came back. I watched her walk back into the room to be alone with Dad. She drove us back home that day, her face streaked with tears, and uncharacteristically for my mother, she didn't say one word to us until she stopped the car outside a shop. Telling us to stay put, she came out with ice cream for each of us and continued driving. To this day, I cannot imagine the strength my mother must have had throughout that time.

Our small country town always pulled together amid any family crisis, and this was no different. Masses were offered and all kinds of cards and packages were sent to our home. It was not for many weeks that we saw Dad again but only after the swelling had gone down and he was in active recovery. Times were hard during these long months as Mam was a stay-at-home mother and my father's garage was the only income we had. Somehow we made it.

Finally Dad came home but was told by his doctors to "take it easy." However, as he reminded us, "Mortgages don't pay for themselves or put food on the table." For the self-employed, the luxury of time to rest often takes a back seat to pragmatism. Life took on a different character during this time. My mother went back to work at a local pub, cooking and tending bar while Dad started work in the garage again. I can't imagine what his first steps back into that space must have been like as he saw the pit where the fire took place. A vivid memory from this time is sitting at the dinner table together and seeing Dad's hands, which had been particularly burned. The new skin that was trying to mend was bleeding through dirt and motor oil, their meaty rawness cracked open; those hands would bleed regularly as he earned a living to support us. Dad never talked about the fire, and in time, we stopped asking him about it. But despite the grave nature of his injuries, my father did make a full recovery and his doctors told us that the fact that he did not need any skin grafts was a small miracle.

The next few years were difficult ones for our family. As I reflected on this time years later, I came to realize that the seed of my prayer life was sown in the suffering of those turbulent years. I sought refuge in quiet places and the fireside chat with Grandmother Hannah and my aunts Josie and Veron, who lived in our same town. I found myself spending time reflecting on the "big" questions in life such as "Where am I going?" "What is my purpose?" and "What lies beyond what we see in this life?" Gradually I become more at ease in my own company and could often be found lying on my bed in the silence for hours. When my mother asked me what I was doing, I often responded that I was "thinking about things." What I was doing, in fact, was praying the *lorica* of St. Patrick. If life seemed chaotic, I realized that the inner sanctum of my being did not have to be. In solace, I learned how to actively cultivate a sense of peace in the midst of the storm. You can too, no matter what the storm looks like, by learning this prayer form.

Pattern Prayers of Protection

Like most children in Ireland, I learned to sing the lorica of St. Patrick in both English and Irish, and it was as familiar to me as the Barry's or Lyons tea that is drunk in most Irish houses. The word *lorica* comes from the Latin word for "a coat of armor, mail, or breastplate" that was put on before the Roman troops would go to battle. The famous "Christ before me, Christ behind me" prayer of St. Patrick is part of a series of prayers invoked for their protection and strength. I drew heavily on this prayer tradition when I stumbled across a box of cassettes in my parents' garage that described the benefits of meditation. At this time, my mother was a heavy smoker, and the cassettes seemed to be part of a smoking-cessation program. The program didn't seem to be working for my mother, but the cassettes piqued my interest because the covers promised "how to learn to cope during challenging times." I popped a cassette into my 1980s boom box and began to listen. I found that I could not turn it off and listened to it repeatedly until I didn't need to listen anymore because I knew just what to do. Each night I began to practice a very simple exercise in the quiet of my room to still my mind and ease into sleep.

Here is the basic formula: Lie down and close your eyes. Visualize your entire body all at one time. Pay attention to your breath, notice its rhythm, and breathe slowly in and slowly out. Then, beginning with your head, move down through each part of your body. Think about your day and picture any tension that is being held in this particular part of the body. Moving down the entire length of your body, exhale all the negative feelings that this part of your body is holding. Pay attention to the small aches and pains in all parts of your body, particularly in your fingers, for example, and the tension behind your eyes. Feel them unbinding and unknotting, and then move on to a different part of your body. As you visualize your heart, synchronize your breathing and feel your breath expand your heart with love. Complete this exercise until you have moved through your entire body; then exhale a final cleansing breath to relax and release. The whole exercise should take no more than a few minutes.

This ritual became part of my regular prayer time when I asked God to help me identify any pain that I was holding on to. As St. Patrick had, I called upon God to help restore the places that needed healing, to release the spaces that needed to be released, and to increase my capacity for love. I found that if I asked God to show me the areas of weakness and tension I was clinging to, I could connect my physical, emotional, mental, and spiritual health more clearly. The stress that I experienced subsiding wasn't simply physical relaxation; I began to seek a sense of total peace in which my mind and spirit felt rested and refreshed. After a few months, my prayer became more intentional. At the end of my nightly meditation and prayer, I imagined, instead of a breastplate of armor, a thin veil of gold settling over my being that protected me from harm and infused my being with the love and light of God. Even though my life became very difficult through these years, my resilience and ability to weather the storms increased. For me, the ritual of praying each night helped to release the negativity and darkness I was holding on to. Sleepless nights gave way to rest, and I found that I could step into the inner chapel of my soul at a moment's notice by slowing down my thinking and instead becoming aware of God's presence.

Prayer is cultivating a friendship with God. Prayer helps us create rituals that ground and strengthen us in relationship to God. Rituals help us move between threshold moments, and their patterns help us navigate through thin moments. Another important Celtic ritual takes place at sacred sites or thin places and is known as "walking the rounds." This involves prayerfully walking "sun-wise," beginning with the east (since Christ comes from the east) and moving clockwise. The number of rounds varies but is often three to reflect the sacredness of the number three in the Celtic tradition—something we will discuss later.

There are also "pattern days," days associated with particular saints in Ireland on which people carried out specific activities and rituals on their feast days. There are pattern days associated with different holy places and a set number of rounds to walk in specific places along with certain prayers. These "patterns" are associated with mental, physical, and spiritual movements that help our temporal bodies keep pace with the rhythm of our eternal soul. The prayer form that I described above is what I call my "pattern prayer" and feels different every time I practice it. I incorporate meditation, reflection, Scripture, spontaneous prayer, and formal prayer, knowing that the author of my prayer time is God, not me.

What I have described here are not new practices. Their roots are deep and ancient. They transcend the popular movements of practicing mindfulness and contemplation and reach back into the ancient world of the early Christian church. If you want to practice this form of lorica prayer, set aside some time each day to ease into it. As we say in Ireland, *tóg go bog é*, or "go easy on yourself," and try your best. Tell God what is on your heart, sit in the silence, and listen to what comes to mind. God will speak when you are ready to listen. Give thanks for the experiences that have led you where you are today and give thanks for the experiences to come tomorrow. St. Augustine of Hippo, a father of the church, reminds us that the past we entrust to God's mercy, the future to God's providence, and the present to his love.

One of the biggest questions that helped me pinpoint the source of my stress during this part of my life was this question: what is the one thing that I want to let go of in order to be truly happy and at peace right now? We may be tempted to list a litany of small worries, but there is usually a root cause or issue that eats away at our ability to live a peaceful and free life. Naming that "one thing" isn't always enough to let it go; listening is the key. That's why rituals are important for us as human beings; they ease us into new ways of being and help us navigate new thresholds of life as they encourage us to listen differently and contemplate time and our place in this time.

At times, we have all wondered if God has forgotten us. My friend Ruth once said, "I don't know if I can hear the voice of God anymore. Even though I set aside time to pray, I don't hear God speaking to me anymore. I feel lonely and abandoned." When we do not hear God speaking to us, we begin to doubt and question ourselves and our relationship with God. We find this silence frustrating and painful. One of the silver linings of God's silence is to highlight for us just how completely and utterly dependent we are on him. When Ruth told me how difficult God's silence was for her, I reminded her how beautiful is her desire for God to be present in her life. Prayer changes us, not God, for we are the ones in need of change. Seeds grow in the silence and darkness of the earth. They are not buried in darkness; rather, they are planted to grow into the light—and so are we. Even though we cannot always see it, the seed of prayer will bloom in love, sometimes when we least expect it.

When you find your own rhythm in prayer, it seems there is no storm that you cannot withstand, and you can hear God's voice, no matter how small and still, as this story from the book of Kings reveals.

In the Sound of Silence

In the book of Kings we read a very interesting story about how God makes himself known to us. The prophet Elijah is told to go out on a mountain and wait for the Lord to pass by. A mighty wind passes by "but the Lord was not in the wind; and after the wind an earthquake, but the Lord was not in the earthquake; and after the earthquake a fire, but the Lord was not in the fire; and after the fire a sound of sheer silence" (1 Kings 19:11–13). As important as words are, silence speaks volumes.

This ability to listen for what is spoken but also for what is unspoken is something that children are particularly good with. Young children are naturally gifted with an ability to see "beyond the beyond" and to approach the world with a sense of mystery and wonder. Young children who cannot read or have limited vocabulary are still remarkably conversant; they navigate the world less through the spoken word and rely more on intuition and their imagination. They pick up context and tone through the interplay of their imagination and attunement. They can sense tension and stress without a single word being uttered. Their imagination can take them out of the ordinary to something extraordinary. A simple cardboard box becomes a pirate ship, and a rock becomes a beautiful treasure.

As we grow up, however, daily living seems to grind down that childlike *joie de vivre* into hard calluses, and we become more cynical and jaded versions of who we were created to be. We laugh less. We become more serious and forget that play is the touchstone of God. Have you noticed yourself become more cynical and less joyful through life? Do you wish that you had some of the energy and sparkle of who you were as a child? Those days might chronologically be gone forever but they are within the reach of your memory. When you appeal to the intellect or the head, you inform. But when you appeal to imagination, you provide inspiration. The world needs inspiration but also information so that transformation can take place. This is the great gift of Celtic spirituality: it brings both together, particularly in prayer.

Prayer becomes a bridge into that space where we draw forth the ability to see the world afresh again like children. That's why listening and giving space to God to speak helps us to be attuned, not just to

God but to others. In the space between our words, God speaks in these "prayer pauses," as I think of them.

I once worked with someone who claimed that he was such an "exceptional listener." The giant eye rolls from his teammates would tell a different story! Even though this person seemed to take in feedback that was offered to him, he rarely acted upon it and often could not recall the conversation later. Many of us mistakenly believe that being quiet is actual listening. But the first step of listening is not just being quiet but tuning in to the other person and listening for what is said and what is unsaid. The first step of listening is to be present.

The Rule of St. Benedict is a book written in 516 by St. Benedict of Nursia. In the opening rule, St. Benedict urges his monks to listen with the "ear of the heart." Deep, empathetic listening is an exercise in attunement and helps us set aside our tendency to listen with the aim of responding rather than the desire to hear what is being said. Prayer is the art of deep attunement and listening—to God and to others. *Prayer is a bridge into thin space.* These "prayer pauses" transcend what is spoken and unspoken but help us connect heart to heart and soul to soul through the space between words. That's why prayer is so important: it helps you come home to the heart of who you are and hits the pause button on the things that are pulling you away from your core.

Many people practice prayer as an exercise in talking to God, but prayer is much more about awareness and listening, as indeed all of life is. There is a Native American proverb that underscores this point: "Listen, or your tongue will make you deaf." In a noisy world where everyone wants to be heard, prayer is even more important because it helps us listen attentively to God and to others. The philosopher Søren Kierkegaard reminds us: "A man prayed, and at first thought that prayer was talking. But he became more and more quiet until in the end he realized that prayer is listening" (as quoted in Richard Foster's *Celebration of Discipline*). Listening to the deepest longings of our heart, listening to the promptings of God for our lives, and listening to the space and pause between words—such listening becomes the space where God and our soul meet.

These "threshold moments" where we cross the space between the sacred and the secular or outside world, between time and eternity, between the spoken and the unspoken, happen all the time. In this regard, the Irish *seanfhocal* is true: God's help is nearer the door and so is our thin place. If you have ever been in a room when someone has passed away or present when a child is born, you get a sense of the movement between the light and the dark that comes with being in the presence of God. Often there are no words to describe what is happening at these moments; they simply take our breath away as we behold the mystery at the heart of the universe.

This is the kind of interior peace that leads us to break free of what people say about us and to attune ourselves instead to the person God is calling us to be. We don't have to go it alone in this journey, though, for we may be gifted with a soul friend or two who navigates the thin moments with us. In this next part of the book, we will move from breaking through to breaking free, beginning with a look at the Celtic gift of the soul friend.

Your Thin Place: A Pause for Prayer

Breaking Open

*Irish seanfhocal (old word): Is giorra cabhair Dé
ná an doras.
Translation: God's help is nearer than
the door.*

One of the central tenets of Celtic spirituality is the nearness of God. Yes, God is powerful and mighty, but he is also intimate and close to us, especially during times of trial. This lovely Irish *seanfhocal* reminds us that God's help is as near to us as the door; it will open for us, all we have to do is ask.

Breaking Through

- Recall a time in your life that was difficult or upsetting. Did you pray during this time? If so, what did your prayer look like?
- What are some of the elements from this chapter that might nurture or even transform your prayer life?
- Name two to three people whom you feel have a strong prayer life. What can you learn from them?

Breaking Free

*By day the Lord directs his love, at night his song
is with me—a prayer to the God of my life.*

—Psalm 42:8

Whether we know it or not, or acknowledge his presence, God is with us by day and by night. This week, set aside some time for silence and prayer. At the end of the week, list three graces that came from this time.

Part Three

Breaking Free

*If you're brave enough to say goodbye,
life will reward you with a new hello.*

—Paulo Coelho

7

Your Soul Friend

*Irish seanfhocal (old word): Ar scáth a chéile a
mhaireann na daoine.
Translation: People live in the shadow of
each other.*

I met Joan at a Celtic spirituality retreat I was facilitating in southern
Wisconsin. During these retreats, many of the retreatants develop life-
long friendships around shared interests and deep conversation. Joan
was an artist who preferred to sketch and draw her thoughts through
the retreat rather than share them out loud. This particular year, I
was leading the retreatants through a component on the Irish concept
of the *anam cara*, or "soul friend." It sparked animated conversation
among the group. Someone in the class posed the question: can you
have a chance encounter of the soul and never see that person again?
Joan, ordinarily so shy and quiet, stepped forward with tears glisten-
ing in her eyes and shared her story.

The Bright Pink Fedora

"It was a rainy Monday, the kind of dreary, rainy Monday that brings
a chill to your bones that only sleep or a hot bath can alleviate," she
began. "I was driving down a street after work when I saw a man
walking. What caught my attention," she said, "were the colors. As
an artist, I often see thoughts in color and people as having particular

colors too. But this person was actually a riot of color. A kaleidoscope of color. He was wearing a purple coat with red rain boots, pants with a houndstooth pattern, and a bright pink fedora. His whole presence drew me to him and smiled to me. I could see the painting of his life with my artist's eyes, and before I could convince myself that this was a bad idea, I pulled my car over, opened my window, and told him to get in." At this point, you could have heard a pin drop in the room, people were so engrossed in the story.

"He looked directly into my eyes, and I felt something inside of myself well up. I could have cried with happiness, which I know sounds ridiculous," she said to the group. "But he got into my car and we drove around the city streets talking and talking and talking. It felt like we had been friends all our lives and had insights bottled up inside of us that we were saving for each other. I felt something come alive in me, and he felt the same. After a few hours, knowing that we had to say goodbye, I asked him where he was going. He asked me to take him to the hospital about a quarter of a mile from where I had picked him up." Joan stopped and picked up a tissue as her eyes welled with tears. "I didn't want to pry but found myself asking if he was OK. He told me that he was going to thank the staff at the hospital for his treatment. He had been given a few weeks to live and wanted to thank the doctors and nurses for taking such good care of him. That morning he put on his best colors to make everyone smile, hoping, he said, 'that someone saw him as he really was.' I held his hands and told him that I saw him, really saw him." Joan cried. "We never said goodbye or exchanged contact information as I dropped him at the door of the hospital. We both knew that there was no goodbye for us."

Joan remembers a day, about seven weeks later, when she knew that her friend had passed. "I don't know how I knew this, but I did," she said, because "I could feel his color leave my soul. My soul mate in a bright pink fedora hat might be gone from the world, but a part of him is always with me."

Joan's story is a dramatic one, but I have talked to countless people whose stories of their soul friend relationships are no less moving and deep. When we get to the core of who we are, our souls will speak their voice, even when we cannot. And if we are very lucky, just like Joan, one day we will recognize our soul friend as one who paints our world with their own colors. In these relationships, we catch a glimpse of just how much God loves us and wants to tend our soul as a friend.

The concept of the soul friend is a rich and ancient one, leading to a deeper understanding of humanity and our walk with God. However, in recent years the increasing popularity of the term *soul mate* has denatured and eroded its essential meaning. Today, it's often written into pop songs and bandied about on television and reality television shows. As a result, it has been reduced to a romantic interlude rather than the deep and abiding presence of the soul relationship that it is. It has become misunderstood and misinterpreted. But the soul friend is a particularly important concept for the ancient Irish and found in many other traditions throughout the world. So, let's take a look, starting with the concept of the soul.

The Friend of Your Soul

The fourth-century philosopher Aristotle, in his masterful work *De anima* (translated as *On the Soul*), makes it clear that the soul is inseparable from its body, for it is the grounding principle of life that animates and gives us life. "It is the source of movement, it is the end, it is the essence of the whole living body," he tells us (415b9–415b11). In Greek philosophy, the concept of the soul friend was written and discussed extensively. In Plato's *Symposium*, for example, he argues that humans have been looking for their soul mate ever since the gods created human beings. Zeus, the central figure of Greek mythology, separated human beings from one entity, thus creating two people. This taking of the whole and separating it in two, or the halves, not only created two distinct human beings but also doubled the number of offerings given to the gods. Those who were separated from each other spent their entire lives trying to find the other person or their other half, so to speak. Many people have surmised that this is where the expression "other half" or "better half" comes from. But we also see echoes of this ancient understanding in the Bible, specifically in the book of Genesis.

The biblical creation accounts described in the book of Genesis are fundamentally different from other ancient creation myths, like the Babylonian *Enuma Elish* (also known as the Seven Tablets of Creation). We are expressly told in Genesis that God created man and woman to be companions to each other: "God created man in his own image, in the image of God he created him; male and female he created them" (Genesis 1:27). However, Genesis features two creation accounts, and one of the accounts specifically mentions the concept of one person being created from another. In Genesis 2:22–23 we are told that God made a woman from the rib of a man, who said, "This is now bone of my bones, flesh of my flesh." At the heart of this account of creation is that the understanding of "bone of my bones, flesh of my flesh" gives way to "soul of my soul," or soul friendship.

In the monastic church that developed in Ireland from the sixth century onward, soul friends had an important place in the Christian community. St. Brigid famously declared that "a person without a soul friend is like a body without a head." Friends would gather and share their confessions with one another routinely and challenge one another on their spiritual deficiencies so as to draw strength from one another. It was not cast in any kind of romantic light but strictly in terms of friendship and faith.

One of my favorite insights on soul friendship comes from St. Brigid, who built a monastic community at Kildare in Ireland. St. Brigid is also associated with the pagan goddess Brigid, and over time, many of the stories of the pre-Christian Brigid have melded with those of St. Brigid. However, we know with certainty that a person called Brigid existed, and the legends, stories, and folktales that surround her all speak to a woman imbued with wisdom, bravery, and insightfulness. Like many Celtic saints, Brigid was convinced that each person needed a spiritual guide who would help them discover and grow closer to God in the ordinary holiness of everyday life. A younger nun named Darlughdach served as Brigid's right-hand woman and *anam cara*, or soul friend.

A ninth-century story written by Óengus mac Óengobann, better known as St. Oengus of Tallagh, called the *Félire Óengusso* or the *Martyrology of Oengus*, outlines the interconnectedness between soul friends in a story he documents from St. Brigid's life.[3]

A foster son of St. Brigid came to see her one day and went to the refectory (a monastic cafeteria of sorts) to get something to eat. St. Brigid asked him if he had a soul friend, and he responded that he did. She told the young man to sing a requiem for his friend because she could see that he had died. The young man was startled, for this was news to him. "I saw when half thy portion had gone," Brigid tells him. Brigid, with her gift for seeing beyond the beyond, could see that part of the man's soul had made its eternal voyage and gone back to its home in the passing of his soul friend.

In more modern times, the Danish philosopher Søren Kierkegaard and the Irish poet and mystic John O'Donohue have expanded the understanding of the soul and put this concept in dialogue with soul

---

3. https://archive.org/details/martyrologyoeng01stokgoog/page/n122/mode/2up/search/ferns

friendship. O'Donohue, for example, describes coming to an understanding of your soul as an awakening and an act of ancient recognition whereby heart speaks to heart and soul speaks to soul.

Relationships That Move at the Speed of Soul

Perhaps you have not thought about having a soul friend until now, or perhaps you already know who your soul friend is. Soul friend relationships are characterized by growing in spiritual closeness, not just in sharing the things of the world. Many women tell me that they have found their soul friend in relationships with each other. Men have told me the same, and several have also confessed their sadness that they feel they cannot talk about their friendship with another man without being labeled negatively. This is a travesty.

Soul friendships transcend ages, race, class, and position, guiding us to break down and break through our fears, sufferings, and triumphs to find meaning and value. They are relationships cultivated by deep respect and empathy, sacred recognition, and connectedness in God. The Celts saw these relationships as fluid like their circles, not closed to each other but open and interconnected. The Celts rejected the philosophy of dualism, with its emphasis on the harsh distinction between the body and the mind, and instead embraced a philosophy of the connectedness of mind, body, and spirit. Soul friends helped connect these bonds.

Soul friends share connections not of their own making but that come as gifts from God. These relationships are a centripetal force that holds us together even when our mental, physical, and emotional health fragments and declines. When we navigate relationships on the basis of what we think instead of from our gut or our souls, we often miss the beauty that lies at the heart of what relationships could be. We make castaway judgments such as "too old," "too young," "different," or "not my type" without even being aware of it. Even before we can rationalize or define what we mean to each other, our souls have already moved to a different space.

Relationships are not just powered by the speed of time but also the speed of soul. We all know that the speed of light is much faster than the speed of sound. The same principle applies in soul friendships. Soul friendships move at the speed of the light of the soul. Even before we can verbalize what we feel, our souls have moved faster than what we can express.

Our souls are the places that hold our light. A soul friendship is the place in which the light inside you meets the light inside the other person. It is the place where those transcendent wisps of light at the level of the soul recognize each other and intertwine. As interconnected and interdependent people, we live, as the Irish say, "in each other's shadows." Soul friendships bring us closer to those shadows in ourselves and in others. Soul friends help to break through the veil between perception and reality and what is seen and unseen. Having a soul friend is not a conscious decision that people make, and many times "you just know" when you have found your soul friend. It is an act of ancient recognition rather than a relationship that you will or choose for yourself. Instead, it is a relationship that is chosen for you by your own soul and the soul of another. An agreement at the level of deep being of the soul that speaks: "This is home, I have found my other half." The Celtic tradition emphasizes that the soul mate is the person with whom we can be completely ourselves—our misconceptions, pretentiousness, and egoism are discarded. We are vulnerable, exposed, and naked, so to speak, but held in loving care and light. This concept of the soul friend, as you can see, is at odds with the popular portrayal of the soul mate regularly depicted in weddings or in magazines. What's the difference? Let's take a look.

"Today I marry my best friend, my soul mate, the one I will love forever"—this statement written on many wedding programs is a beautiful one but misses the mark. You might marry your best friend, or soul mate as popularly understood, but having a soul friend has very little, if anything, to do with romantic love. Romantic love can obscure how objective we can be when it comes to our relationships. We lose the ability to step back and recognize our own spiritual blind spots. Soul friends hold up a mirror to each other's spiritual blind spots and transcend thresholds and thin times as spiritual travelers and sojourners. The expression from my Nanny "You can't read a book if it is an inch from your face" is a good one when we think about the concept of the soul friend. If the concept of the soul mate implies romance, then it is quite different from the spiritual growth that soul friends are called to tend in each other.

After years of speaking about the topic of soul friends, I do occasionally meet someone who has married their soul friend. Is it possible? Absolutely. But it is not as common as the media would lead us to believe. A few years ago, I was teaching a class on this very subject when a pretty, red-haired young woman raised her hand and asked, "Do soul friends always know that they're soul friends?"

"What do you mean?" I asked.

"Well, do both people have to agree that they are soul friends, or is it OK if just one person feels that they're the soul friend of another and the other one doesn't?"

I have to tell you that she asked this question in between sneaking furtive glances at the handsome man who sat beside her! He looked at me with a red face and, with eyes as round as dinner plates, conveyed with every inch of unspoken dignity that he definitely did not feel the same way about the woman beside him. Friends they might have been, or perhaps something a shade deeper, but the idea of him being a soul friend to the woman was certainly news to him! She, however, appeared oblivious to his discomfort and looked absolutely crestfallen when I talked through some of the characteristics of soul friendships.

There are other questions that I get asked quite a bit in relation to the soul friend.

Is the soul friend a mutual act of recognition?

Yes. Both people know it, just "feel it" and click. There is a sense of alignment that could not be an act of either person willing the relationship.

Do soul friends communicate on any other levels? Can they "feel" when good or bad things happen to the other person?

The answer is as varied as the different kinds of soul friend relationships. In short, some do, some don't.

Can you have more than one soul friend?

The soul friend occupies a central place in someone's life. While it is certainly possible to have more than one soul friend, it is highly unlikely given the investment of time and energy needed to sustain the relationship.

Should you pray to encounter your soul friend, or is it better to simply wait for God to bring this person into your life? There is certainly nothing wrong in praying for a person you have yet to encounter. But mutual recognition is at the heart of soul friendships. Rather than pray to meet this person, pray for the gift of divine recognition that God may help you to see and be present to this person when he or she comes into your life.

Do you still remain friends even when one person has died?

Yes. Time is but a brief interlude for soul friendships. What has been joined together, soul to soul, will one day become whole again. Our bodies are mortal, but our souls are not, which brings me to the concept of the immortality of the soul.

The Voyage of the Soul

The old Celtic proverb "he, she, and thee, all things in three," which is a nod to the mystery of the Holy Trinity, is at the heart of Christian relationships. There are three people in every relationship, even when there are only two people who are physically present. Who is the third person? It is God. In the Bible we are reminded that "where two or three gather in my name, there am I with them" (Matthew 18:20), and every time we speak to someone, God, who is deepest within us and is in our midst, is deeply present to us. God is present to us body, mind, and soul. One of my favorite philosophers, Gabriel Marcel, remarked in many of his writings that to love a person is to say to that person, "You, I love will never die for I love you in God who is deepest within you."

Your soul is the spark of the divine. It is the seed of God's immortal love for you. Each of us has that spark, as we talked about earlier in this book. As we are created in the image and likeness of God, or what is called in the Christian tradition *imago Dei* (in the image of God), God's image is imprinted on each soul, incarnated, so to speak. The word *incarnate* comes from the Latin and means "in the flesh." In the Scriptures we read that "the word was made flesh and dwelt among us" (John 1:14). God became man in the incarnation and through Jesus Christ entered our lives in all their messy glory through flesh and bones. God is incarnate in our relationships through Jesus Christ, who lives and walks beside us every day. This relationship is in itself a thin place where the divine and our humanity ebb and flow in and out of each other. Many times we struggle to recognize this thin place, and soul friendships guide us in navigating this voyage of the soul. In many ways, soul friends help us to put "skin and bones" on God as we voyage through life together.

This theme of voyage has been picked up in a classic Irish song made famous by the folk singer Christy Moore. The song uses the metaphor that life is an ocean and when two people work together to create a life, they can weather any doldrums or storms with patience and hope. The chorus is beautiful:

Life is an ocean, love is a boat
in troubled waters, keeps us afloat
when we started this voyage, there was just me and you
now gathered round us, we have our own crew

The lyrics "we have our own crew" can obviously mean children, but at a deeper level it can mean the new life that comes when we navigate a thin place together as pilgrims. This journey is a physical, mental, emotional, and spiritual journey that brings us in and out of thin times, and we are blessed if we are sent a guide or soul friend to row with us through whatever weather.

Soul friendships are spaces in which God is deeply present to us in our thin times. In God's love we never die, for the love that we share is of the divine and, as such, that love is eternal. Soul friends teach us how to love and how to live, but they also teach us how to pass from this life into the next, where our souls are immortal. In this way, soul friends are midwives of the soul, helping bring to birth God's plan for our lives and into thin space.

A seed of immortality is present in soul friendships, and the strength of the relationship lasts even beyond death. Souls don't exist in time and space as our bodies do, and so they find their communion with God beyond what we see in the here and now. Several cultures around the world have strong feelings about messages being sent from loved ones beyond the grave in the form of pennies from heaven, feathers, animals, or birds such as cardinals and robins. Native Americans, for example, believe in spirit animals, and the ancient pre-Christian Celts believed in the transmigration of the soul. Julius Caesar writes in *De bello gallico* that the Celts believed that the soul did not die in bodily death but that the soul lives on and may take another form.

As Christians, we believe in life everlasting. Jesus himself, in conquering the grave, teaches us that one day we will live eternally with

God, the ultimate friend to our soul. As such, our souls are inde-
structible, for they are the spark of life within that exists much like
a memory but even deeper, like love that is shared or a story that is
told. Once someone passes, the love doesn't evaporate or disappear
but lingers and lives on in the memory of the heart and in the recesses
of the soul.

When I think of the concept of the soul friend it is the last verse
of the song "The Voyage" that I often think about, as it references the
eternal nature of relationships:

> Together we're in this relationship
> we built it with care and to last the whole trip,
> Our true destination's not marked on any chart,
> we're navigating for shores of the heart.

One of the most important gifts that a soul friend gives us is their
ability to help us find our voice and tell our story. This is a true act
of breaking free. Our soul friend helps us to break free and find our
voice so that we can share our story with others. It is to our own story
that we now pilgrimage together.

Your Thin Place: Your Soul Friend

Breaking Open

*Irish seanfhocal (old word): Ar scáth a chéile a
mhaireann na daoine.
Translation: People live in the shadow of
each other.*

We live in the shadow of each other. Those we love can shield and shelter us. The old Irish concept of the soul friend teaches us that some people will have a deep and lasting bond. We do not exist alone but walk together as pilgrims.

Breaking Through

- Do you have a soul friend? If so, what qualities drew you to each other?
- If you do not, do you believe that it's possible that you have yet to meet this person? How might you recognize your soul friend?
- What are the most important aspects of soul friendship?
- What are the most misunderstood aspects?
- Have you ever had an experience of the soul that was fleeting, yet that moment or encounter has lingered for you through the years?

Breaking Free

*The Lord God said, "It is not good for the man to be alone. I
will make a helper suitable for him."*

—Genesis 2:18–25

Being alone and experiencing loneliness are not the same thing. The first person we live with is ourselves, and if we can befriend our own person and be hospitable to our own voice, we will find, in conversation with God, that we will rarely be lonely. This week, share a soul conversation with a trusted friend and tease out some of this chapter's implications for your relationship.

8

Finding and Telling Your Soul Story

Irish seanfhocal (old word): An té a bhíonn
siúlach, bíonn sé scéalach.
Translation: He who travels is full of stories.

On the bus coming home from a party, Joel, who was in the row behind my friend Janet and me, leaned over and asked, "Hey, Janet, I don't know you very well. What's your story of faith?" That question took a lot of guts, but it took even more nerve for Janet to admit: "I've never thought about that before. I don't know if I have a story, much less a story of faith." Many people have said the same thing to me. But trust me on this: every single person has a story of faith.

Your Soul Story

Nobody is ever lost to God, no matter how far we might stray from him. No story is insignificant or unimportant. Have you ever lost someone you love? Had your heart broken? Thought you couldn't get out of bed to face one more day? Been let down? Had moments that took your breath away? Didn't recognize the person who looked back at you in the mirror? If you have had any of these experiences, you have a soul story.

And because you are a person, you have a story to tell.

All our relationships and experiences are threads woven together creating the most beautiful tapestry of story—our soul story.

Soul stories are the stories we often keep hidden from others because, like Narcissus, we find it much easier to stay at the surface. I call these surface stories "glory stories" because of their tendency to focus on only the positive ending. "Ta-da!" they exclaim "I did it, my life was a mess, but look at how it all turned out: perfect!" While it is easier to skip to the parts of our story that have been redeemed and made whole, the real value comes in allowing others to see inside the cracks of our story where we were broken open: the thin places. Our story is the bearer of our joy but also our pain, or to put it another way, our "soul scars" that time and faith have mended or are still mending. Like the ancient *seanachai*, or the bearer of "old lore" in the Celtic tradition, we are a bearer of old lore in our own story.

Word to the Wise

Human beings are at heart storytellers. We are so drawn to telling and living in story that at night our stories continue in dream format. The art of storytelling is at the heart of all cultures, and the Irish too have a long tradition of oral storytelling. The Irish, like many Celtic groups, are highly verbal, passing down legends, stories, and tall tales from one generation to another. For example, even though the Celtic tribes scattered throughout Europe had an understanding of Greek, they did not commit their laws, histories, and religious beliefs to writing but passed them down orally from one generation to another. In Caesar's *De bello gallico*, he mentions that the Celtic high priests (known as Druids) spent as long as twenty-nine years in training, during which time they committed to heart the folklore, laws, rituals, and practices of their ancestors.

This tradition lives on to this day in the *seanachai*, or those persons entrusted with the art of storytelling or bearers of "old lore." The *seanachai* is often imbued with a wisdom that comes from observing people and from building or dissipating tension or humor through storytelling. Like many Irish children who go to the pub on an occasional Sunday with their family, I relished the opportunity to have a bottle of Coca-Cola and a bag of Tayto chips in the village pub. The pubs and hearths of Ireland are fertile ground for music, mischief, and the magic of storytelling. Stories are swapped from family to family, intermingled with legends, myths, and, quite frankly, "blarney."

As a child, I was often described as having "the gift of the gab," which is a common enough occurrence in Ireland. Adding that gift of gab to a keen memory and a love for history, I participated and won many *seanachai* competitions in my childhood. Reading mythology, history, folklore, and fairy tales kept me busy for hours on end, and I was often described as a bit of an old soul because I soaked up stories like a sponge.

My mentor was a wise old lady who had a flair for the dramatic and a gift for long bardic-style recitations. I used to cycle out to Vera's house for practice, and she, along with my mother, would coach me on intonation and the art of dramatic presentation. With Vera's mentoring, I competed in the All-Ireland *seanachai* competitions, taking second place in the national competition when I was sixteen. From the stage, I saw firsthand the power of words to hold people captive, to draw forth emotion, and to unite people in grief or humor.

Even today, the millions of people who travel to Ireland to see the famous Book of Kells or the ones who view it digitally are a testimony to how language captivates and connects us. So powerful is the ability of story and words to shape culture and civilization, that they have been the subject of destruction but also great preservation throughout the ages. The word was sacred to the Celts and the great founding traditions of the world, and it should be just as sacred to us too.

A common greeting when meeting someone in Ireland is, "What's the story?" which means "What's going on?" or "Have I missed anything interesting?" In Dublin, many times it is even abbreviated to

"Story?" as a greeting and way of catching up. The phrase comes from the Irish expression *cad é scéal agat*, which literally means "what story is on you?" Story helps us to see ourselves, others, and the world differently. Children too have this great gift of story, although it is not often nurtured as it should be. My godmother, when meeting a baby for the first time, would declare, "That one has been out before!" She meant that the child, though newly born, looks with the eyes of the wise upon the world. Story is at the heart of who we are as people, even if we sometimes forget the art of good storytelling.

The Power of the Word to Harm and Heal

Words hold tremendous value for shaping our worldview and contributing to how we perceive ourselves and others. Consider the great lengths that people throughout history have gone to preserve the written word. After the collapse of the Roman Empire, the European monks fled from the attacks of various tribes who burned their way through ancient libraries and priceless manuscripts. At great risk to their lives, they safeguarded treasures and antiquities and brought them to Ireland and the British Isles for safekeeping. Countless works from the ancient world, including those of Aristotle and Plato, were preserved for future generations by those monks. During World War II, many Jewish people valiantly attempted to preserve the sacred texts of their faith, which were sought out by the Nazis for burning and destruction. These texts were sacred and intrinsic to the identity of the Jewish people, texts that anchored them to God, to their history, and to each other. Censorship still happens today in many parts of the world, proving the old maxim to be true that "the pen is mightier than the sword."

Just as language evolves constantly and is shaped by continually changing cultural and societal forces, new words are constantly entering conversation. Twenty years ago, nobody would have had any idea what a "tweet" was all about or how to write a "Facebook post."

However, with the evolution of connectivity, we are also losing the beauty of certain words and their meanings. Consider the word *memory*, for example. In the past, the only frame of reference for this word was the human context, but the word *memory* now applies to devices such as a computer, a phone, even a washing machine. Words are in danger of being stripped of their relational context as we navigate the "real" and the digital world, which can often dehumanize relationships. There is power in words—to heal and transform but also to denigrate and debase. Healing words are like droplets of water that come together as a river of story for those who listen to its music.

A poem that speaks to this reality is one that I learned in grade school and that has stayed with me. It is entitled "Truth" by Barrie Wade:

> Sticks and stones may break my bones,
> But words can also hurt me.
> Stones and sticks break only skin,
> While words are ghosts that haunt me.
> Slant and curved the word-swords fall
> To pierce and stick inside me.
> Bats and bricks may ache through bones,
> But words can mortify me.
> Pain from words has left its scar
> On mind and heart that's tender.
> Cuts and bruises now have healed;
> It's words that I remember.

If information is power, then words are its currency. We see this today in the scurrilous muckraking that goes on in political campaigns that hurl words at people and use them to deceive and destroy. Words can be a balm for the soul or a weapon of mass destruction when they are directed at entire groups of people and used to marginalize and dehumanize them. Consider the experience of the Irish—and many other people throughout the world—who have clung to their native tongue in times of trial and persecution as they were often prevented from speaking their own language or practicing their faith. There is a lovely expression coined by the Irish teacher, barrister, and national hero Pádraig Pearse: *Tír gan teanga, tír gan anam*, which means "A country without a language is a country without a soul." If that is true, then a person without a soul story is a person without a voice. Let's look at how to identify and share our soul story.

Story as Thin Space

How many times a day are we asked how we are doing, and how often is a trite greeting at the grocery store or workplace such as "How are you?" met with the automatic response like "Fine" or "Just great"? If we would stop and look someone deep in the eye and ask, "How are you really doing?" we would realize that this question is an invitation to a story. Listening creates the sacred ground where story can emerge.

Each of us has our own way of seeing and describing the world, but for pilgrim beings, finding our own voice is a necessary step for our own spiritual growth. Giving voice to who we really are is an act of powerful vulnerability in a world that wants to airbrush relationships, experiences, and people. Finding our story and telling our stories are acts of great courage and authenticity. We can all "smell a lie," especially when it comes to story.

The phrase "telling stories" has both a positive and a negative connotation. In Ireland, when someone is accused of "telling stories," the person hearing the story suspects a lie. Tracy Chapman, in her poignant song "Telling Stories," pokes at this tendency to hide the truth even when we are telling our own stories. She sings of the lies we tell ourselves between the lines of space in our memories. Our truth and "the truth" are not always the same.

Telling your story is not just breaking down what happened to you or how you broke through. Story is not just about the mechanics of what happened but instead about why it happened and how we have been shaped by the experience. It is a sad truth that you can tell your own story without sharing who you really are. People can sense when you are being authentic and when you are not. You can share your experiences without giving yourself over to the listener. But sharing your soul story is deeper than that.

Story is the ground of thin space. Your story is your journey in and out of the thin spaces in your life. It is a trusted exchange of soul meeting soul and how God pulled you, dragged you, or carried you to where you are today. Soul friends have an important part to play in helping you curate experiences and identify the most impactful movements in your story. But even if you do not have a soul friend, you can certainly find your soul story through reflection, discernment, and prayer. Entering your story is a thin place as God and each one of us work together to journey through the spaces between our memories.

Giving voice to the real, messy, heartbreaking, and authentic "you" is an act of breaking free from what others think about you and even what you think about yourself. If you find identifying and sharing your soul story challenging, you're not the only one. I resisted doing this for years, but once I had laid out my story, I felt that I had broken free of many of the lies I had lived out. I was broken open, and a deep sense of peace settled into my bones. God's presence in my life through those times of intense suffering became clearer. Even after my husband and I endured difficult seasons, such as when our daughter was diagnosed with a chronic illness, we never doubted God's presence in our lives or our love for each other. He was the first person that listened to my story and cried with me, knowing no words are necessary when there is an outpouring of pain. This was a thin place for both of us.

Sharing our soul story is a gift both for the storyteller and for the listener, for it is in the sharing of our stories that communal bonds are strengthened, relationships are deepened, faith is nourished, and

God's movement in our lives is revealed. This is a thin place in which words seep into our subconsciousness. A single word can transport us to a place in our memories, either positively or negatively. Just as in Plato's myth of the cave, where the people were physically chained together, words can also chain us to our own cave. Those who have been in abusive situations often find that the words linger far longer than even the pain of physical or sexual abuse. Many times, the words that were hurled at us become the words that haunt us, in our waking and in our sleeping. As we journey through life, it is important to stop and examine the voice inside our head because unchecked, negative thoughts become negative attitudes that become negative behaviors.

Perhaps you haven't thought about the specific words that are a regular part of your speech and how they have shaped your understanding of who you are and how others see you. We approach the world through our senses, and our language often reflects this. My friend David approaches the world many times through his intellect and finds himself using language such as "I know what you mean" or "Help me to understand why you think this way." Others approach the world through the visual and use words to reflect this, such as "I see what you mean" or "Help me to see more clearly what you mean." Those who approach the world through the affective or their heart will sprinkle "feeling" words throughout their conversation such as "I feel your pain" or "I just feel it in my gut." Those who approach the world through their sense of hearing will often pepper their interactions with expressions such as "I hear what you are saying" or "I hear the emotion in your voice." Those who are tactile will generally use metaphors drawn from the material world to ground their conversation in concrete and tangible ways. Sometimes we will use a combination of all these figures of speech but very often find our comfort in one dominant modality.

Soul Space

"I just need some head space," my friend Ethan told me. "A place where I can just breathe and where I don't have to make any decisions." Many of us feel the same. But if creating head space is important for mental health, then the concept of soul space should be just as important. We need to create ample time for reflection and silence, which are necessary conditions so our souls can breathe, especially given how we rely so much on words to communicate. But words are obviously not our only form of communication. Space helps too.

Many people today, especially young people, are drawn to story but not so much to the written word. Social media platforms such as Instagram are a testimony to how popular storytelling is, but in this case with images rather than words to tell stories. We are hardwired for story, and we have come full circle in how we tell them, as today we also use etchings, drawings, and images. But lest we think this is a new phenomenon, we should consider how our ancestors told story through images—in the cave paintings of Lascaux in France or the hieroglyphs of ancient Egypt. But as important as the specific words or images are, so too is the space between them. The monks of ancient Ireland inherited Latin manuscripts to translate in their scriptoria and noticed that all the Latin words ran together on the page without any spaces. To make the words easier to digest, the Irish monks inserted pauses or spaces between the words to help the reader breathe into the text. The gift of the space between words is one of the Irish monks' greatest gifts to the world, and it has a lot to teach us, spiritually speaking.

As we put one foot in front of the other through life, we need to make sure to pay attention not just to the words that people say but also to what is unspoken and unsaid. The pauses are where the nuances of conversation lie, the space where the breath of God can be listened to and where the ordinary and the extraordinary come together. We can discern thin places in our lives only if we are open to listening for them.

The gift of space between words is not something we should ever take for granted, especially when it comes to sharing our soul stories. In the silent space between words, a depth of feeling and emotion is conveyed that allows the listener or reader to enter the story by connecting memory to the present and reality to the perception. In sharing our story, particularly our journey of faith, vulnerability, sensitivity, and trust are all on display.

When we forget who we are, we forget our story. Nobody can live your story for you, and even if we occasionally allow others to write parts of our story for us, it remains our story. When we strive to live out someone else's story, we live an imitation of what it should be. Your story is as unique as your fingerprint. And yet the storyteller remembers that, at heart, each of us is connected and our stories are intertwined. Stories become a part and parcel of family life—talking about our ancestors can take us back eight hundred years in a single conversation! Stories speak to the place in our memories that shapes our understanding of our home. When we draw from the wellspring of story, we draw into it our family, our circle of friends, and the wider community in which we dwell. All stories are shared stories. When your story becomes my story, ultimately it becomes "our story" as people of faith.

God is the author of life and, in a very real sense, the author of each of our stories. If he provides the pen, then we supply the ink in our experiences. The pen and the ink come together as an act of divine creation as we write our story with God together. Every day is an opportunity to begin anew, for each day is a page and each week a chapter in the story of God's love for us. Soul stories are the thin places of our own dying and rising to new life, which is at the heart of our human journey that we will now explore.

Your Thin Place: Finding and Telling Your Soul Story

Irish seanfhocal (old word): An té a bhíonn
siúlach, bíonn sé scéalach.
Translation: He who travels is full of stories.

Breaking Open

Far from being a literal translation of expressions such as "travel broadens the mind" or "he [or she] who travels knows much," this expression reminds us that story allows us to travel into the world of another, whether we tell them ourselves or whether we hear them from another. While traveling undoubtedly broadens the mind, so does journeying through story. Story creates thin spaces where we find meaning and common ground with others.

Going through life will always bring challenges and opportunities. Choose two to three thin places in your life that have defined you. These may be experiences in which you felt that your life was moving too fast or you were being pulled away from the core of who you are. Of these two or three experiences, which one was the most impactful for you? Start with this experience.

- Did you have a breakdown moment or series of breakdown moments? What happened?
- Where was God in this part of your story? Where was your thin place at this time?
- What was in the junk drawer that you didn't want to deal with at that time of your life? Name it and claim it.
- What one word or emotion describes this time of your life?

Breaking Through

- At some point during your experience, darkness turned to light and there was a breakthrough. You entered a thin place. This period is marked by a renewed energy and vigor for life.

- Identify the turning point. What was this moment or time like for you?
- What was the threshold that you decided to cross during this time?
- Name two to three things that helped you break through this time.
- What did your relationship with God look like at this point in your journey? What did this thin place feel like?

Breaking Free

Breakdowns that are followed by breakthroughs very often lead to "breaking free" of people, events, experiences, or behaviors. As time eases the wounds of what transpired, we recognize that our pain has not just been transformed but transfigured—from something sad and dark to a rich and deeply meaningful season of our lives. This period is marked by acceptance and peace.

- Identify what freedom looks like for you on the other side of this story. How are you different? How are you the same?
- Where did you see new life in breaking free?
- Where did you find renewed confidence in yourself?
- Where did peace and acceptance come from during this time? What did it feel like?
- Who or what helped you become more open to God's presence?
- If you were to sit with your eighteen-year-old self, what advice would you give to this person, knowing what you know now?
- What do you believe to be the central message of your soul story?

Let the redeemed of the Lord tell their
story—those he redeemed from the hand of the
foe, those he gathered from the lands, from east
and west, from north and south.

—Psalm 107:2–3

9

From Dying to Rising

Irish seanfhocal (old word): Nuair a thiocas an
bás ní imeoidh sé folamh.
Translation: When death will come, he won't
go away empty.

As the clouds parted, I got my first view of Ireland's legendary patch-work quilt of green fields. It was a beautiful Friday morning, but my heart was heavy. Just a few days before, Mam had called me. "It's time to come home," she said, breathless. "It's not going to be long now." Leaving my husband and two young children behind, I flew back to Ireland. My mother was dying, and I didn't want to believe it.

Taking a Turn

She met me at the kitchen door in her pink bathrobe, and although I could see how much she had declined, she looked strong, and I was hopeful. *Perhaps she's wrong*, I thought. "Let's go have a cup of tea," she said. So we sat outside on her patio drinking tea, catching up on news while she pulled out a pack of cigarettes. I was shocked. Mam had given up smoking ten years earlier. "I took it up again," she said, "to deal with the stress." I "gave out to her a bit" (an Irish expression meaning scolding) and told her that she needed to take care of herself more. She looked at me with what I know now was pity and kept on smoking. That weekend saw a flurry of activity as neighbors popped in bringing flowers and gifts for my mother; she turned fifty-four that Sunday. We celebrated with my aunt Veron, singing to my mother as we gathered around the table and toasted to her life with champagne. Through these days Mam maintained good conversation but got tired in the afternoon and would sleep for a few hours before she would get up again and putter around in the kitchen or the garden.

On Monday, Mam "took a turn." It was barely noticeable to most of the family, but something in her spirit had shifted. I could sense it but couldn't put my finger on what it was. Dr. Phelan, the only family doctor we had ever known, came to examine Mam on Monday. "Your vitals are all good, Angie, your heart is strong, you are breathing well, and I think you look good," he remarked. "I'm off on holidays for the rest of the week but will be back next Monday," he told her. "Ah, I don't think so, Dr. Phelan," she answered from her bed, "I won't be alive by then, I'll be dead on Friday." Both Dr. Phelan and I were shocked. "Now, now, Angie," he told her, "you will be grand, I'll see you next week." And he patted her hand. She gave him the same look that I had received when I told her she needed to give up smoking.

On Wednesday morning, Mam was still in good spirits and going up and down the stairs slowly by herself. But a visit from her friend Catherine on Wednesday afternoon alarmed me. Catherine is known locally as "the washer woman." Part nurses, part wise women, Catherine and her friends often arrive when someone in our town passes away. They will often wash and clothe the body of the dead so that the family are spared this task in their grief. The "washer woman" has been an important part of Irish culture, although this too is changing.

"How's she doing?" I whispered. "It won't be long now," she told me. Death has its own secret knowledge, I've learned, a language known only to those who are as comfortable with the process of death as they are with life. Those who know its secrets can see nuances of the body changing color, breathing change, and eyes losing focus.

Those who are comfortable with death see what is coming before the rest of us do. This was all a foreign language to me. I thought that Catherine must have been exaggerating, because that evening, my sister and I gave my mother the facial she asked for, plucked her eyebrows, and painted her fingernails and toenails. Mam looked good and was cheerful.

But Thursday came and she didn't get out of bed but drifted in and out of sleep. I lay beside her for three hours that day. "Are you afraid of me?" she asked a few times. "I'm not, Mam," I told her, but we both knew that I was afraid, afraid that death was coming for her and I couldn't stop it. Midway through the afternoon she woke up and said, "Julianne, do you see that young man over there? He's just over there by my chair." There was nobody there.

"Ah, look," she said, her voice softening. "He's lovely." I sat up on the bed beside her and leaned in as her voice was faint. "Julianne, make sure to tell Nicola that he's happy and lovely," she said and then fell fast asleep. Nicola was a young woman who was a good friend of our family. The summer before, her son Rian had passed away from cancer at the age of six. My mother used to visit Rian when he was sick, and I believe that on this day, Rian as a young man came back to see my mother.

I walked down the stairs to the kitchen to get a drink and there sitting at the kitchen table was Nicola. I almost had a heart attack! I told Nicola my mother's message and watched the tears stream down her face. Nicola visited with my mother while I sat and tried to think through what was happening.

Awhile later, I went back up to Mam's room. Although her eyes were closed, she could hear me and had moments of lucidity. At one point in the afternoon, I told her that I loved her. When I was back at home in America, I called Mam often, and at the end of the call we would say, "I love you." But it was a kind of rote statement rather than a fact.

"I love you, Mam," I said. "You were a good mother." I didn't expect her to respond.

"Was I?" she asked. I held my breath.

There it was, the ultimate question hanging in the air. Time slowed down.

The years of sadness, anger, and anguish I had felt toward her all fell away as I looked into her eyes and said, "You were."

We continued to look at each other, and our eyes were opened as we really saw each other. We saw what we were to each other and what we had become to each other. We looked at each other, perhaps for the first time in years, with unconditional love.

In this shared gaze, no words were spoken, but in my heart I told Mam that she did the best that she could, and I could feel her response in my soul. "I'm sorry," her eyes said.

"It's OK. I'm sorry, too," I said as I held her hand. She fell back asleep. Peace settled into our bones and we lay at rest. It was my last conversation with her.

Friday was my youngest brother's twenty-first birthday, the "love child," as my parents jokingly referred to him. We were looking forward to celebrating James's birthday by Mam's bedside with all our family. That morning I gave her a kiss before I went to pick up my husband and our two children from the airport. She mumbled that she heard me, I hugged her, and I left the house. My husband had driven four hours to Chicago and then braved one of the world's busiest airports and an eight-hour flight all by himself with two wiggly babies. Relief washed over me when I saw them walk through the barrier at Dublin airport. I kissed each one of them what seemed like a million times and inhaled the sweet baby fragrance of my daughter Ava, who was not even one year old.

We were twenty minutes from home when we got the call. Mam had taken her last breath.

She did indeed die on a Friday, just as she had told us she would. She had passed on to her eternal home.

Wild Country Roads: Take Me Home

For many years, I struggled with the concept of home. The word *home* carried within it a split reality: it was where I lived but not where I wanted to be. As an emigrant, I had one foot planted in Ireland and one foot lightly touching the soil of America. Going home to Ireland was tinged with the joy of seeing family but also the sadness of watching others' relationships deepen and grow—relationships I had once been part of but was part of no more. My old life in Ireland had gone, people had moved on and, I realized, moved on without me. To be sure, I was still a part of the family, but the old adage was true that out of sight can be out of mind when you live three thousand miles away. I felt orphaned, but I couldn't name it for many years, and then one day it struck me: I didn't know where home was. In the longing to "be" home, I realized that I didn't "belong" in the same way anymore. Longing and belonging are rooted in each other, often painfully so. This time of my life was very difficult, and to this day I can feel the scar tissue of the wound that remains. Each one of us carries scar tissue like this. Regardless of whether we leave our country, we all go through this pain. Leaving home for the first time, taking our children to their first day of school, watching our child go to college, losing a loved one—for us, home and belonging are being redefined all the time.

The longing for home is very much a part of the fabric of American life. American society is a fondue pot of all different cultures, languages, and religions mingling and melding. It's what makes America great: the ability to be enriched by the lives of others. Almost 32 million Americans claim Irish ancestry, which is astounding when you consider that the population of Ireland has hovered around 4 million or 5 million for more than one hundred years. Often when I meet new people and they hear my Irish accent they tell me, "I'm Irish too." When I ask when they lived in Ireland, they often reply that they have never lived in Ireland or even been there, but their great-great-great-great-great-to-the-eighth-grandfather emigrated from Ireland to Mississippi in the 1600s. When this happened the first couple of times, I was puzzled. "How on earth," I asked myself, "could you grow up in this country all your life and yet consider your identity and home to be a completely different place?" But now I understand.

A few years ago, I had the pleasure of taking a group from the Midwest to Ireland for a pilgrimage. The distinguishing feature of a pilgrimage, as we have discussed, is that you enter the culture, spirituality, and traditions of people through the lens of faith. You begin to appreciate all the elements that shape a culture and not just appreciate the beautiful buildings or the friendly people but enter their sufferings, joys, and triumphs. Pilgrimage puts the pilgrim in touch with the soul of the country.

For those with Irish ancestry, this coming home was visible even on their faces. The pressure and pace of regular life was left behind as we transitioned to Ireland, a place where time is secondary to experience and presence. Something in the soft greenness of the landscape and the cadence of the language soothed these pilgrim souls, and they settled into Ireland as "home." One lady told me, with tears in her eyes, that journeying to Ireland for the first time helped her understand who she was at the deepest core of her being, and she began to see herself much differently.

What and who we call home can gnaw at our hearts unless we make peace with it. A longing for home is more than just longing for our place of birth or where we grew up. It is a longing for a place where we belong. Home is the touchpoint of our memory.

Our need to be and to belong is at the root of our longings for home. The song "Take Me Home, Country Roads" by John Denver speaks clearly to our longing to be home and to belong. As we sing the phrase "to the place I belong," it reveals a universal longing to belong. Belonging and longing-to-be are interconnected.

The heart tug for this place called home never goes away, and it's important to acknowledge this. Home is less a physical place and more a space in your heart and your memory. It doesn't matter where or who we call home, but each of us ought to spend time thinking about how our understanding of home has affected us and will continue to affect us throughout life.

Home is not just a place but a journey. This yearning for our true home is at the deepest longings of who we are. No matter where your ancestors are from, your sense of home as being "other" or "right here" is an important part of your story. My mother's passing gave me the gift of peace. When I finally let go of my expectations for what I wanted home to be, I finally made peace with the concept of home. From a small village in the Wicklow Mountains to a home by the shore of Lake Michigan today, home speaks differently to me today. The Irish proverb is true: "Your feet will bring you to where your heart is." We have a home for now (our temporal home) and a home for later (eternal). We will always be betwixt and between these two places, the place where our feet are and the space where our soul belongs. This tension for defining our home ebbs and flows throughout our lives, shaped by those we love and those who refuse to love us, those we live with and those who have passed on to their eternal life. I know that in my eternal home I will see my mother again.

Rising Again

Mam died on a Friday, her wake was held right away, and she was buried on the third day, as is the Irish custom. Three days. The triple cycle of life, death, and resurrection all at work together. Mam wanted everything done, as she said, in "the old way," and so her wake and funeral were of a traditional sort, even if her life was not. The Celts believed that after a person's death, the soul needed a clear path so it could travel unencumbered to the otherworld. This is why all windows and doors are kept wide open when a person dies in Ireland.

After my mother passed, the window of her bedroom was opened to allow her soul to leave peacefully out the window. All the clocks in the house were stopped and all reflective surfaces were covered, including mirrors and television screens, so that her soul could make its way unencumbered from her earthly home to her eternal home.

These practices and similar ones are widespread in many parts of the world, not just Ireland, and they can make us uncomfortable because they are often at odds with Christian practices, but in Ireland they are rooted in tradition and custom. When I asked my sister why she stopped the clocks (even though I knew the root of the Celtic belief), she responded, "I don't know, that's just what we do here." This "just what we do here" carries the memory of practices that stretch back to pre-Christianity, and even if the reasons for them have been lost, many people still cling to them, especially in times of trial.

On the day that Mammy died, the bells rang from the town church as they do upon the passing of any resident. The undertaker came with a coffin for my mother. It entered the house "head first" so that when my mother was taken away she would leave feet first from her home. When she left, the house was thoroughly cleaned and our living room was turned into a funeral parlor with chairs laid out in a circle around the room. When Mam returned, she was laid out in an outfit of her choosing and with rosary beads intertwined through her fingers. Flowers were placed all around the casket and the windows were all darkened. Candles were lit to illuminate the darkness of the room, which harkens back to the old Celtic belief that the demons of the darkness could be held at bay by the power and light of fire. Mam was propped up slightly, with the bright fingernails that she had asked us to paint winking at us.

And then they came. Hundreds and hundreds of people to pay their respects. Buckets and buckets of tea were served as people came and sat by the coffin. On Saturday my lovely American husband complimented my sister on the food and asked where she had ordered it from. We both laughed. "Just watch," she told him. And he did. Every time someone came into our home, they brought with them plates of sandwiches and biscuits, pieces of homemade Irish Christmas cake (which lasts for a year for there is so much whiskey in it). And the old bachelor men who could not cook? Well, they brought with them bottles of "good" Irish whiskey, which people drank neat or added to the tea. Some told stories, the rosary was prayed, and sometimes music was played. We laughed, we cried, we cried, we laughed. As is the Irish custom, the body is never left alone at the wake and so the family take it in turns to stay with their loved one, praying and saying goodbye.

Many customs around death and dying have their roots in the ancient world, and many cultures throughout the world observe a three-day process of death and burial. The day between the death and the burial is often the hardest, for the silence of the tomb stands between life and eternal life—just as it did for Jesus, just as it did for my mother. Sometimes the one who has passed away will be brought to the church for a prayer service the night before their burial. They are left in the church on their own that night to "make their peace with God in the silence of the tomb," as one old woman from my village told me. But that is not how my mother wanted it. She stayed at home for two nights until the day of her burial. She was afraid to be in that church on her own for reasons that she did not share with us.

On the day of her burial, our family followed behind the hearse to the church, pausing only outside her childhood home, her last chance to make peace with her parents and our ancestors, already gone on to their graves. Shades were drawn on homes and businesses, and people stood outside their homes, heads bowed, older men with their caps in their hands. My father wore the suit that my mother had left out for him the week before. She knew that he would not have the presence of mind to pick out a suit with a matching shirt and tie, and so she had neatly pressed everything, polished his shoes, and left it all in a special place where he could see it.

Mam's funeral service was beautiful, and we were given a surprise right at the end. My mother had left school at the age of sixteen but had continued taking the occasional class to qualify to go back to college. For her fiftieth birthday she enrolled in college and was two years into her degree in social care when she was diagnosed with cancer. Of all the things that my mother had to endure, she cried bitter tears when she could no longer go to college because she was so sick. However, the president of the college stepped forward to speak about my mother's keen love of learning and told us that she would indeed receive her degree, posthumously, among a very select group of people to receive such an honor since the college's founding in 1793.

After the service we stepped out into blustery conditions, and people rushed forward to share their condolences and say the customary greeting of Ireland following a death, "Sorry for your troubles." I witnessed so many people weeping for my mother, and in that moment I realized how death resembles an orchestra. In the orchestra of life, the tune and music that I associated with my mother was one musical instrument, one note: her identity as my mother. Many times the music she played sounded discordant to my ears. But upon her passing, I saw the instrumentation of her life come together with music so profound and sweet in the voices of those who told me their stories of the music of my mother's life. "Your mother gave me my first job." "When I ran away from home, your mother found me and told me everything was going to be OK, and it was." "When I was kicked out of my home as a teenager for having a baby, your mother came and showed me how to bathe my child." "Your mother visited me when my daughter committed suicide. She sat and let me cry." On and on the music played.

The rain was driving and harsh. But we stood together and walked the mile to the graveyard where she was laid to rest. We could hardly hear the words of the priest, so loud was the wind that whistled around us. But as her body was placed in its waterlogged hole, the wind died down, the rain stopped, and a faint rainbow was visible.

I looked up and thanked God. She was at peace and her soul was home at rest. And my soul was at peace too. We had navigated our own thin place. We had broken free.

Your Thin Place: From Dying to Rising

Breaking Open

Irish seanfhocal (old word): Nuair a thiocas an
bás ní imeoidh sé folamh.
Translation: When death will come, he won't
go away empty.

Irish seanfhocal (old word): Is iomaí lá sa chill
orainn.
Translation: We are in the churchyard (grave)
many a day.

Both these expressions are translations of the idea that death comes to all of us.

But in the Irish language there are interesting linguistic quirks and idiosyncrasies, such as in the second expression, *is iomaí lá sa chill orainn*. Note the use of the preposition *orainn*, which means "on us." This is reflective of a different Irish perspective regarding the person and his or her experience. One defining characteristic of Irish is that, unlike many languages, it has no separate words meaning "to have" or "to want." In Irish, people and their conditions or their experiences or even their names are not one and the same. For example, the term *tá brón orm* could literally be translated as "I'm sorry," but the most appropriate translation is "sadness or sorrow is upon me." Sadness, just like death, will come upon us but also will pass from us.

Breaking Through

- Is there a relationship or experience to which you want to die and rise again?
- What does breaking free look like for you?
- What do you think of when you hear the word *home*? Where do you feel most at home?

- How does this sense of home help you understand who you really are?
- How is the place where you belong (and long to be) a thin place for you?

Breaking Free
*I have fought the good fight, I have finished the
race, and I have kept the faith.*

—2 Timothy 4:7

This week, spend some time thinking and praying about someone in your life who has passed away. Harvest from that relationship, even if it was a contentious one, two to three lessons you are grateful for. Write them down and give thanks for the person that shared these lessons with you.

Part Four

Coming Full Circle

Irish seanfhocal (old word): Is maith an scéalaí an aimsir.
Translation: Time is a good storyteller.

10

Creating a Space for Grace,
Part I

*Irish seanfhocal (old word): Ní neart go cur
le chéile.
Translation: There is no strength
without unity.*

In every crisis we learn just what we are made of. While we cannot
change what happens to us, we can change how we respond: we either
grow closer to one another or farther apart. Popular culture pushes
the narrative that we are independent of one another, but as we've
learned from the COVID-19 pandemic, along with every other crisis,
we are interconnected and interdependent. In just a short time, the
way we lived, where we prayed, and how we grieved and celebrated
all changed. Together we witnessed acts of great bravery and courage
from those on the front lines who sacrificed to keep us healthy, safe,
and stocked up with essential supplies. We also witnessed unrest,
rage baiting, and what one middle school student called "flame wars"
that gnawed away at our peace. We have recognized that all life is
sacred and connected in what the Canadian philosopher Charles Tay-
lor refers to in his writings and interviews as "webs of interlocution."
What we do affects the whole in the circle of life.

Creating a space for grace in your life is an especially important
practice in helping us respond to whatever life throws at us. Drawing

from the wisdom of the Celtic spiritual tradition, I want to emphasize five core practices of grace to help you create a space for grace in your life, your own thin place if you will:

G—Grow in gratitude
R—Release regrets to rest and reset
A—Authentic availability and acceptance
C—Cultivate radical hospitality
E—Embrace simplicity

When God is at the center of your life, you will find that your life becomes a space for grace, a space where your soul finds its rhythm and can peaceably move from one season to another. Within this space, we are free to create, bless, grow, and break open. The space is not limiting but flexes, changes, adapts, and accommodates. When we live in this space, there is a thinness in our interactions and no separation between the sacred and what is often referred to as the secular.

In this chapter, we will explore the first three practices and in the next chapter we will explore hospitality and embracing simplicity.

Grow in Gratitude

Blessings and invocations are an integral part of Celtic spirituality. Even today, it is not uncommon in rural areas, particularly in the west and southwest of Ireland, to find people who speak their prayer life in the rhythm of blessings. The language of Ireland is rooted in spirituality by which faith and culture intersect with religion, and it is a deeply incarnational language. The word *incarnate* embodies the spirit in human or bodily form, and this can be seen in how the Irish acknowledge one another in Gaelic. Our typical greeting in English is to say "hello." The same acknowledgment translated into Gaelic (which the Irish people simply call Irish) is *Dia Dhuit*: "God be with you." This greeting reflects the divine spark within each person. The traditional response to this form of greeting is *Dia is Muire Dhuit*, which means "God and Mary be with you." God and his mother, Mary, whom the Irish often call "the Blessed Mother," are to be honored together.

The history of Ireland has always emphasized the strength of women and their contribution to the world. In pre-Christian Ireland there existed myriad goddesses and gods that the Celts worshipped. Morrigan is one such example. In the Brehon Laws (a series of Irish laws that were stamped out by British rule around the early seventeenth century) the equality of the sexes was emphasized, and there is ample evidence of matrilineal policies whereby land and certain positions were passed through the female line. The male and female characteristics of life are acknowledged and held in balance together.

The phrases "God bless" and "good health" were my grandmother Hannah's typical greetings and farewells to us as we came in and out of her little house. When I asked her why she peppered her hellos with "God bless" and her goodbyes with "good health," she responded that those who were very poor often passed along blessings for good health and God's blessings because it was "all we had to offer." Although my grandmother spoke only English, there is no doubt that somewhere in her speech patterns she had picked up the old Irish expression *Slainte mhor agus a h-uile beannachd duibh*, which means "Good health and every good blessing to you!" She may have lost the memory of that proverb, but clearly her tongue had not!

Another distinctive feature of the Irish language is the marking of time through the language of devotion. The words for Wednesday (*Chéadaoin*), Thursday (*Déardaoin*), and Friday (*Aoine*) speak to the liturgical practices enshrined by the ancient Irish. Many Irish people in times past would fast on Wednesdays and Fridays, so the Irish word for Thursday, which is *Déardaoin*, means "the day between the two fasts." The heart of blessing is gratitude for the other. One of the most beautiful Irish expressions is still found in the Irish word for a person with a disability: *duine le Dia*, which translates as "a person with God." Those who are differently abled are afforded a dignity as we acknowledge God's special presence in their person.

There is a beautiful Celtic tradition that honors the seed of gratitude and pays it forward in the form of blessings to others. Blessings for making the bed, baking the bread, bathing children, and cleaning the house are all a part of the Irish language. Speaking blessings throughout your day reminds you of the goodness that is all around you and also within you. Blessings are always rooted in gratitude. Gratitude is the memory a sincere heart holds on to when life is difficult. The converse of a blessing is a curse, and there are plenty of examples of curses found in the Irish language. Some are humorous, such as *go dtuitfeadh an tigh ort*, which means "your house will fall upon you," but some are more ominous, such as *go mbrise an diabhal do chnámha*, "that the devil will break your bones," or *lagú cléibh ort*, meaning "weariness of heart upon you."

While the idea of someone cursing us or wishing us harm might seem a bit far-fetched, it often happens to us more than we realize. Some years ago, my coworker Katherine walked into my office and told me she had been withholding in our relationship for some time. "For a few different reasons, I decided not to like you," she confessed as she settled into the chair opposite me. "So instead of seeing you as a coworker, I saw you as a competitor. But what I realized," she said, "is that you had no idea that I felt like this. But I recently heard you talking about the Celtic custom of blessing and cursing others, and I knew that's what I had been doing. I have been withholding blessings from you, which was my way of cursing your happiness and joy." As you can imagine, this was an emotionally charged conversation, but we came to a place of acknowledging and seeing each other, perhaps for the first time, and we committed to working on our relationship.

Our world would be transformed if we lived out of our blessings rather than our curses. When we withhold goodness toward others, live with a spirit of envy in our hearts and the sharp words of gossip on our lips, we curse rather than bless. John O'Donohue reminds us that blessings draw a circle of light around a person that protects, heals, and strengthens them. A grateful heart is the seed of the flower of transformation that will bloom in our hearts if we are sincere. Blessings are not utterances or platitudes but prayers of the heart lifted to God from a space of goodness. Related to the practice of blessings is our second practice of grace, which frees us from those curses that we hold on to and allows us to rest and reset.

Release Regrets to Rest and Reset

As we have talked about many times in this book, the interconnectivity of our mind, body, and spirit cannot be underemphasized. What we think affects how we live, and what we believe in our heart affects the depth of our soul. Even today, in various parts of Ireland there are "faith healers" who bring together physical, emotional, mental, and spiritual ailments in their practices.

Cures for various ailments were passed on from one family to another in Ireland and many Celtic nations. In ancient Ireland, Celtic physicians, known as *liaig*, enjoyed high legal status in society, being one of the Gaelic learned orders. Women known as *bean feasa* or "wise women" may no longer be as common as they once were in Ireland, but they still can be found, if you know where to look. The interconnectedness of body, mind, and spirit is masterfully expressed in this Irish poem, which was written anonymously:

> It's not your back that hurts, but the burden.
> It's not your eyes that hurt, but injustice.
> It's not your head that hurts, but your thoughts.

Not the throat, but what you don't express or say with anger.
Not the stomach that hurts, but what the soul does not
     digest.
It's not the liver that hurts, it's the anger that's inside.
It's not your heart that hurts, but love.
And it is love itself that contains the most powerful
     medicine.

What we hold on to can weigh us down. Clinging to fear makes those fears larger and gives them a voice, a voice they shouldn't have. One of the keys to breaking free from your fears, as we have already explored, is moving from the dark into the light. Releasing regrets is one of the keys to interior freedom and peace. Making peace with ourselves is often a lot harder than making peace with others as it is often our own thoughts or regrets of the heart that imprison us. "We are not slaves of the past, nor masters of the future," an old *bean feasa* told me. "We are servants of the mystery that is unfolding in the here and now."

To be a servant of the mystery means opening your heart, eyes, mind, and ears to God, who surrounds us in all that we do and in all that we are, right now, in the present moment. We are not masters of a future of our own making but servants of a mystery beyond our comprehension, beyond our imagination. To be a servant of the mystery means recognizing our brokenness, imperfection, and lack of wholeness—and acknowledging the same brokenness and imperfection in others.

Did you ever drive on a highway or interstate and notice how many messages are competing for our attention? One of the first things my eye noticed when I emigrated from Ireland to life in Wisconsin was the noise of American life. Noise isn't just what we hear but also what we see. Despite the rural nature of the town we lived in, the highways and streets were often cluttered with billboards, flashing lights, and signs. Even when we are driving, a time when we are supposed to be focused on the road, the neon signs create a "noise" that can drown out our own thoughts and reflections. It seems that everything is competing for our attention, time, and money.

When every element of daily life is filled with noise, there is no time for silence or contemplation. At home in Ireland, despite the winding and twisting roads, we drive from place to place largely uninterrupted by the flashing of commercialism. The roads themselves, with their border of hedgerows, are carved from the natural paths that people have traveled for centuries. This allows your eye to wander over the landscape naturally and provides fertile ground for the imagination and the release of contemplation to take over. If we enter the natural world, not to shout or dominate, but as a partner, we will be able to find ample spaces in which to rest. Rest does not mean "doing nothing." Working with ingredients from the natural world—the materials of gardening, for example—takes us out of ourselves so that we can connect with the earth again. One of the best resting spaces for me is bread baking.

Our Daily Bread

When I was growing up in Ireland, homemade white bread and brown bread were table staples. Irish soda bread is a hearty, stick-to-your-ribs kind of bread that carries you from one meal to the next. Despite the trends that demonize bread and gluten, I still eat bread every day, and one of my favorite smells is the scent of fresh-baked bread wafting through the house. My grandmother Hannah baked the most delicious soda bread, which I've never been able to replicate, and so, in addition to Irish soda breads, which do not use yeast, I make yeast breads and sweet breads every week.

Baking is a creative art in which seemingly random ingredients come together to create something new and different. The act of bread making is therapeutic and multisensory. In contrast to the feel of a computer's keyboard, which is hard and fairly uniform, baking uses your hands differently, and you come into intimate contact with each ingredient. Yeast is alive and responds to the conditions and other ingredients around it: heat, fat, acid, and sugar. Too much salt or heat will kill yeast, so you have to be careful. When you knead bread, you learn how to break down the proteins in the dough so that it becomes elastic and pliable. Experienced bakers come to a point in the kneading when they will tell you that they "just know" when it's done. If the dough is under-kneaded its structure will be hindered, and it will not hold together and rise well in the oven. Kneading too much will damage the proteins in the bread, producing a small, dense, flavorless loaf that might collapse onto itself. You want to knead until the dough "springs back" when touched. Once you have your dough ball together, you do something very important: you leave the dough to rest. During this time, the complex proteins in the dough relax and the air bubbles work their way out, thus increasing the elasticity of the dough and developing the flavor.

Baking bread has a lot to teach us about living, rising, and dying to ourselves. The ingredients of our lives can seem haphazard or happenchance, but they are not. All the ingredients of a life come together to create something new and beautiful with time, care, and the right conditions. Yeast is the living organic principle, the soul of the bread. It can be damaged and impaired by the wrong conditions or ingredients. With a bit of warmth and sweetness, the yeast of our soul can bubble up and enliven everything around it. With a bit of intentionality and a hands-on approach, our lives will result in a bread that nourishes others and ourselves. The mixing, kneading, and shaping processes are just as important as the ingredients.

The relationship is clear between kneading and needing. If our needs are not met, just as with the bread-making process, we can become tough and never rise to our opportunities or challenges. If we are too needy, we can collapse in on ourselves, damaging ourselves and the other ingredients of our relationships. When life stretches and pulls us, we develop the ability to spring back and be resilient. Too much pushing and stretching, however, can cause us to collapse in on ourselves. The most important principle that ties all of these together is the ability to rest. Bread cannot rise well unless it has rested well. And neither can we. Even between the crucifixion of Jesus on Good Friday and the Resurrection on Easter Sunday, Jesus rested.

Just as our bodies and minds need rest, so does our spirit. Rest doesn't mean mindlessly scrolling on social media or simply becoming inactive. Rest is not simply about the absence of noise or distractions. It is a soul state in which our body is in pause and our mind is at peace. Rest is part of our daily bread. You cannot rise unless you rest, and unless you rest, you cannot rise. So, rise and shine!

Our next grace practice flows directly from our ability to rest and reset.

Authentic Availability and Acceptance

Rest allows us to reset and see ourselves and others in a more loving light. When we are too highly strung, worn down, or exhausted, we miss opportunities to embrace the experiences or people who are good for us. We become pushed to our limits—of our patience, our time, and our energy. When it comes to our experiences or a particular season of life, we tend to think in terms of duality: good or bad, happy or sad, bitter or sweet. But this leads us to miss the nuances and shadows that lie at the heart of every encounter and every season. The tendency to segregate people and experiences always leads to division, compartmentalization, and fragmentation because it forces us to think in absolutes: black or white, right or wrong. Throughout history, we have witnessed the tragic effects of segregation by race, creed, and ethnicity, and the scars of segregation still run deep in the memory of many countries, especially the United States. Segregation goes against who we are as human beings. When an us-versus-them mentality becomes enshrined in policy, injustice and dehumanization are at work. As human beings, we are capable of so much more than fragmentation and separation; we have the ability to hold nuance and fragility in tension, as enduring winter seasons in Wisconsin taught me.

Living in Wisconsin, I have come to (grudgingly) accept the frigid winter temperatures because the rest of the seasons are so beautiful, even if they are short. Winter eases its icy grip on the land when you least expect it, and we have often been surprised by a late April or early May snowstorm. I used to dread these farewell kisses from Old Man Winter until I learned to accept them and make peace with the unexpected beauty that comes from them. A fresh blanket of snow transforms and coats whatever it settles upon, and the quietness allows your eye to pick out nuances you may have missed before. One day as I walked in the quiet of the winter beach, I looked at the snow, so pure and white earlier in the week but now intermingled with the beige sand. I was lucky enough to capture a picture of this interplay of shadow and light, of intermingled snow and sand. Some might have said that the snow looked brighter and cleaner in its purest form, but as it gave way to the sand, the sand added depth and shadow to the snow. The landscape was no longer monochrome but textured, with highlighting and contours transforming the ordinary into the extraordinary. This was a great lesson for me in how God works even through the most painful experiences.

During childbirth I initially found myself resisting the pain of the rising contractions. I would tense up my whole body, but as I found out the hard way, the pain only intensified. It was when I leaned in and faced the pain head-on that the labor progressed quicker and I found relief. Tough times always birth newness. When we are pushed to the edge of our limits—of time, patience, energy, empathy, or compassion, we can lean in to acceptance and let the soul lead the way.

The second part of availability is the challenge of acceptance—of ourselves and others. When we are more easily able to accept our own failings, we will in turn be able to accept more easily the failings of others. The natural world teaches us this too.

Bend Like a Reed

Going to the river to swim with my cousins was one of my favorite things to do in the summer. My aunts Josie and Veron lived in the same town as us, and so we all would meet up at the river to spend lazy summer days. Picnic fare was simple: sandwiches, packets of Tayto Crisps, and hard candies for a treat. I remember the taste of homemade jam sandwiches shared among my twelve cousins and the luxury of the occasional jam and banana sandwich. Bottles of cold water or what we called "minerals" (soda) were tied to a rock in the stream to keep them cool. There were no distractions, video games, or phones during those days, just the pure joy of being together and playing in the water.

Every living thing that cooperated with us became a part of our playground. We climbed the trees on the riverbank on the "deep side" of the river and jumped into the river to cheers and catcalls from friends and family. We caught tiny fish—we called them "minnies"—in small nets and kept them in buckets for observation or bait, releasing them before we went home. We used to play with river reeds, blowing through them and bending them into all kinds of shapes. One day, my mother pointed out to me that few trees grow in the middle of fast-moving rivers. They usually grow on the riverbank, and there is a good reason for that. If the force of the river is too great, the tree and its firmly anchored roots will snap and break, she explained. The reed, by contrast, though much smaller and thinner, will survive a raging current because it can flex and bend to accept the rush of water. It is the quality of flexibility that the reed depends on to survive. The tree stands rigid and tall, great qualities for other landscapes but not in the river, where its rigidity becomes a source of weakness. Thus, reeds are mostly found in the water where they can flex, and trees are found on land where they can anchor their roots.

This analogy has a lot to teach us when it comes to accepting others and ourselves. When you are faced with a torrential downpour or find yourself in the middle of a rapidly moving current, reed-like flexibility and adaptability are smart survival strategies. Acceptance and adaptability are always linked. During the 1960s, W. Ross Ashby, a British cyberneticist and psychologist, proposed a law with regard to levels of variety and regulation within biological systems. It is known as the law of requisite variety. Ashby proposes that if a system is to be stable, the number of states of its control mechanism must be greater than or equal to the number of states in the system being controlled. What this means is that, to cope properly with a variety or diversity of problems or situations, you need to have a multiplicity of responses equal to or greater than the problems you face. You need to be flexible and adaptable. Rigidity offers us only one way of seeing and behaving, whereas acceptance gives us a multiplicity of options.

I've already mentioned that my husband works with those who experience various forms of addiction. He gave me some very helpful advice regarding acceptance and adaptability. He calls these principles the 3 Cs:

1. You cannot *control* others.
2. You cannot *change* others.
3. You cannot *cure* others.

These 3 Cs help us maintain a sense of perspective so that we can flex and see people and situations differently. When it comes to difficult people, rigidity of thought or behavior is unlikely to be helpful and can hurt us and others. Far from giving up control in these kinds of situations, we actually gain more from the situation by our adaptability. There's a joke that the only people who like change are babies with wet diapers! But the reality is that we are in the midst of a river of change all the time. Change is a part of our DNA, and yet we resist it in order to be comfortable.

Spiritually speaking, rigidity narrows our thinking and our ability to bless and accept the river of change. Those who are rigid thinkers often cling to surety and unmovable principles. They eschew tension in favor of comfort. But flexibility and resilience are linked, for they help us appreciate the present and move with the current. Although there are times when we must stand firm like a tree and speak our truth, authentic acceptance of God's plan for us and for others is always open to the grace of God.

In the next chapter, we will look at two further practices inspired by the Celtic tradition to help us continue to create that space for grace.

Your Thin Place: Creating a Space for Grace, Part I

Breaking Open

*Irish seanfhocal (old word): Níor chuaigh fial
riamh go hIfreann.*
*Translation: No generous person ever went
to hell.*

*Irish seanfhocal (old word): Ní neart go cur
le chéile.*
*Translation: There is no strength
without unity.*

While we cannot literally know if there are generous people in hell, both
of these expressions remind us that generosity of heart, spirit, and action
is always rooted in care for others. This is what it means to be united.
Accepting ourselves, warts and all, means that we will be more likely to
accept others despite their faults and failings. Life is not a uniformity of
thought, behavior, or belief but rather is a unity, and there is no strength
without unity.

Breaking Through

- What are you most grateful for at this moment?
- What is one concrete thing you can do to be rooted in gratitude?
- In your own life, what connection do you see between kneading and needing?
- How do you release regrets?
- How flexible are you in your personal life? Your relationships? With others? At work?
- In your style of relating to others, are you more like a tree with fixed roots or a reed that can bend? What about in your relationship to yourself?

Breaking Free

For I am gentle and humble of heart and you
will find rest for your souls.

—Matthew 11:29

- Take the time to count five of your blessings right now.
- Be thankful for the present moment and the person in front of you.
- Start listening more to understand rather than to respond.
- Start a gratitude journal or storyboard to remind you of your blessings.
- Leave time to be free from noise and distractions each day so that God can speak to you in the silence of your heart.
- Practice the art of flexible intentionality: be intentional about the values by which you live, but learn to adapt and accommodate others.
- Get outside and appreciate the beauty of nature.
- Bake. Read. Walk. Garden.
- Give thanks for your golden soul scars.
- Believe the best about humanity and continue to trust in the goodness of the Lord.

11

Creating a Space for Grace, Part II

*Irish seanfhocal (old word): An té a thabharfas
scéal chugat tabharfaidh sé dhá scéal uait.
Translation: Whoever will bring a story to
you, will take two stories from you.*

What a journey we have been on together! Throughout this book, we have worked hard to break down our fears so that we could break through to find our voice and be free of the noises and distractions of the world. We have tackled different areas of our lives, looked at centrifugal forces that have disrupted the natural rhythm of our souls, and identified other practices that have helped us create a space for grace in our lives inspired by the wisdom of the Celtic tradition:

G—Growing in gratitude
R—Release regrets to rest and reset
A—Authentic availability and acceptance
C—Cultivate radical hospitality
E—Embrace simplicity and silence

In this final chapter, we will focus on the last two core practices beginning with radical hospitality, for which the Irish are so well known.

Radical Hospitality: Gathering as *Meitheal*

In secondary school, I went to an all-girls school called St. Leo's College, run by the Sisters of Mercy. St. Leo's is part of a leadership program called *Meitheal* (pronounced "meh-hill"), which forms ten students to be peer leaders who are an intermediary group between the school staff and the student body. At the core of this training is the focus on Micah 6:8, which asks, "And what does the Lord require of you? To act justly and to love mercy and to walk humbly with your God." It remains to this day one of the best examples of a prayerful supportive community I have ever experienced.

Although the concept of *meitheal* might seem new to many of us, it derives from a much older concept of supportive fellowship that is intrinsic to the Irish way of being in community. *Meitheal* is a practice that is essential to many farming communities and is practiced organically in many cultures and traditions.

When I take groups to Ireland, my preparation of the group always involves an attunement to the landscape. "Pay attention to what you see," I remind the groups. "Let the landscape speak to you and jot down any things you notice that seem out of the ordinary or unusual." A common question that comes up from pilgrimage groups is why sheep in the same field will have different colored markings on them. I explain that the colored markings differentiate between various landowners in areas where there is common grazing and where sheep owned by different farmers will mingle together.

My friend Mattie is a sheep farmer, and one day as I was out with him on his tractor, I asked him why he allowed his sheep to wander from field to field, all over the mountain. "How will you know if they are sick or need to be moved somewhere else, especially during dipping season?" I asked. Dipping season is that time of the year when sheep are moved or "dipped" through a concrete trough of water mixed with special chemicals to remove all kinds of bugs and bacteria from their fleece. "Well, when it's time for dipping season," Mattie said, "I give the lads around here a phone call, and we decide what day we are going to dip the sheep. We get together at the pub and look at a map of the whole area and decide which areas we are going to cover. So I might take the upper eastern corner of the land map and then I simply go out and round up all the sheep in that area, it doesn't matter who owns them," he explained. "Then I take all the sheep to my dipping tank and dip all the sheep together—so my sheep are dipped with the Whelans' sheep and the Murphys' sheep. By the end of the day, I know that my sheep have all been dipped. The Whelans and Murphys have dipped mine as I have dipped theirs. It's that simple," he said. "No need for a list or a meeting, just a phone call, an agreement, and a pint of Guinness and a small glass of whiskey after the job gets done." He laughed.

What Mattie talks about here is a living example of the old Irish custom of *meitheal*. The word itself doesn't translate well to English but loosely means "working group" or "gathering." Usually, *meitheals* came together out of dire necessity: for example, bad weather meant that crops had to be harvested quickly, or a farmer's barn might have been in danger of collapsing so a *meitheal* was formed to save it. There was a silent agreement that underpinned the *meitheal*: you graciously labor to support your neighbor, knowing that your neighbors would then come through to help you in your time of need. In many neighborhoods across America, the concept of *meitheal* is alive and well, but in other neighborhoods, people live side by side without knowing who lives on the other side of the fence or the wall.

The practice of *meitheal* is an antidote to the sterile individualism that commercialism and materialism push upon us. At the heart of *meitheal* is the spirit of joyful hospitality—of receiving the "other" as family—and it is this practice of radical hospitality that nourishes the soul.

Making Room for One More

The Irish expression *céad míle fáilte*, meaning "a hundred thousand welcomes," is at the heart of Irish life. The Irish have always been famous for their hospitality, and this has undoubtedly contributed to the worldwide success of the "Irish pub." The secret ingredients of this success are the basics of welcoming: radical hospitality, hearty food, good drink, and honest conversation. It is this practice of radical hospitality that sets the table for an encounter at which God can be present to every person and minister through each small act of kindness. Radical hospitality makes each person feel the embrace and warmth of a sincere welcome, devoid of judgment, narrow parochialism, insularity, or separatism. It is this practice of hospitality that helps us break out of our own isolation and welcome another as friend. It's an attitude that affirms, "Yes, there's always room for one more person at the table" or for a new idea, because we are called to be hospitable, not just to new people but to new ways of thinking and, indeed, living. Hospitality makes way for the unexpected, as my grandmother Hannah would say: "There's always an extra potato in the pot, sure, you never know who is going to turn up for dinner." Sometimes we did, but many times we did not.

My father employed various workers in his garage through the years who came home with him for lunch and dinner. I never questioned why Harry, my dad's right-hand man, came home for dinner each night, even though he lived in the same town as us. He worked with my dad and therefore he ate at our table. When Harry got married, my dad was in his wedding party, and when Harry had his first child, my dad became a godfather. "As thick as thieves" my mother once humorously characterized their relationship. Many times, others came for dinner without any advance notice at our house. The modern formality of calling someone to "invite them to dinner" was unheard of when I was growing up. If you were hanging around with someone and it was time for dinner at their house, regardless of whether it was your dinnertime or not, you ate at their table or they ate at yours and somehow everyone was fed. "Potatoes do that, you know," Nanny once said to me with a wink. "They just magically multiply in the pot." Just like the miracle of the loaves and fish in the Bible, when Jesus and the disciples fed the multitudes with just five loaves of bread and two fish, the miracle of hospitality is that it multiplies gifts of love and generosity without us even being aware of it.

Hospitality is another one of the hallmarks of Celtic spirituality and flows from the belief that a spark of God resides in every human being. Generosity and hospitality are linked; opening your door or your home begins with opening your heart to receive and embrace. For the Celts, turning somebody away from your home or your table was considered seriously sinful, worthy of receiving the same lack of welcome from Christ himself. I once heard an old woman share an ancient prayer that emphasizes this principle beautifully:

> O King of stars!
> Whether my house be dark or be bright
> It will not be closed against anybody;
> May Christ not close his house against me.

Christ may come in the guise of a friend or a stranger but, nonetheless, should be welcomed into the heart of the home. In Hebrews 13:2 we are reminded "not [to] forget to show hospitality to strangers, for by so doing some people have shown hospitality to angels without knowing it." It took a few years for my husband to accept the open-door policy of our home, with people showing up out of the blue and staying long into the night. But he became accustomed to it after his first trip to Ireland when he saw firsthand the practice of "visiting": neighbors popping in for a cup of tea or to borrow sugar or some flour, relatives who just happened to be passing by and stopped in for a chat or what we affectionately call a "chin wag"—all are the unexpected blessings and sometimes the frustrations that come with embracing a spirit of hospitality. It was this spirit of hospitality that I extended to my neighbors, and within a year, our culture of "Midwest nice" had been transformed into a community where the spirit of *meitheal* reigned.

With the practice of hospitality, boundaries will be tested as we exercise sensitivity to the rhythm of another person's life, not to mention practicing common sense. Turning up at someone's house at nine o'clock for a "natter" or chat may sound like a good idea, but you may have to hold that thought until the morning until you can test the waters. Hospitality is never neat and easy. It is an art more than a science, but the practice of hospitality is never wasted and in fact always multiplies in its own way. Cards left on our doorstep, packages filled with the blessing of homemade preserves, candy, bread, and little thank-yous are some of the ways we have been surprised through the years. We have been given far more than we have given away through these interchanges.

The Celtic saints were well known for embracing the sacred bonds of hospitality and extending that practice not only to friends, family, and strangers, but also to animals. St. Brigid of Kildare was known for welcoming strangers to her community with a mug of beer and an "oat cake." She welcomed animals too and is often portrayed with a plump goose in her arms. St. Kevin, the famous hermit monk of Glendalough (which is close to where I grew up), was praying one morning and a blackbird landed in his outstretched hands. So afraid was Kevin to disturb the birds that he allowed them to make a nest in his hands during the season of Lent. The legend tells us that the eggs hatched on a bright Easter morning and flew from Kevin's own hands. Hospitality becomes a space where, like St. Kevin, our own hands become a space to cradle new life.

The practice of radical hospitality transcends boundaries of race, religion, sex, and culture. It speaks its own language and is given, not for any reward or gain, but freely out of a spirit of love. It is this spirit of love that we must always put forth, because the first place we practice hospitality is where we extend it to ourselves. Before we can extend hospitality, we ought to reflect whether we are hospitable to ourselves. It's true that you can't give what you do not have. Extend generosity and hospitality to yourself by ministering to yourself with the care and devotion you extend to others. The summary at the end will help you work through some helpful practices.

Related to this practice of hospitality, and one that helps balance the business of hospitality, is the opportunity for us to embrace simplicity and silence. Earlier in this book, we have explored the value of silence, but I want to introduce a few related concepts regarding simplicity in terms of visual noise and clutter that take this concept even further.

Embracing Simplicity and Stillness

Can you identify some of the happiest times of your life? Choose one to focus on right now. Can you tap into that memory and remember that feeling? Name that feeling right now.

For me, I have a memory of playing "swing ball," also known as "tetherball," outside as a child with my sister during the summer. My memory holds on to the simplicity of the time, a time with few expectations or demands, a time filled with play, a time of true joy. When many of us think back to times in our childhoods, even if there were difficult or traumatic experiences, there were ample moments of simplicity in which we felt more creative and freer than we had before—or since. The practice of simplicity is not just for children but is a deliberate and conscious choice in how we live today.

Some years ago, when Pope Francis was elected pope, he caught my heart with his focus on simplicity of life. Here was a man who, upon being elected as head of the largest single denomination in the world, bowed his head and asked for a blessing from the people as a servant of those same people. He wore only a white cassock and simple black shoes, eschewing the trappings of the modern papacy by refusing to wear the red cape with furry trim and the red shoes of his predecessors. After being elected pope, images of Jorge Bergoglio riding the subway back in his native Buenos Aires were combined with images of him as Pope Francis boarding a minibus after the conclave and paying his own hotel bill. Pope Francis was intentionally communicating to the world that his papacy would emphasize a church more focused on intentional simplicity and even poverty than on grandeur and pomp. It is a message that has resonated with millions of people around the world, for it acknowledged the stranglehold that clutter and material goods have on all of us.

In homes across America, it seems that many people are on a mission to declutter. Even with a typical uptick in January donations, thrift stores reported an increased surge in donations during the COVID-19 pandemic. Fueled by the popular success of books and TV shows emphasizing decluttering our physical spaces, it seems that we are examining our relationship with material possessions, and with good reason. Based on a rigorous, nine-year project at UCLA, scientists working with UCLA's Center on Everyday Lives of Families studied a number of families with regard to their lifestyle, possessions, stresses, and trials. Their findings appeared in the book *Life at Home in the Twenty-First Century*. What they found is a cautionary tale in terms of how society has become fueled by materialism, business, overscheduling, and stress. Among their findings:

- America has only 3.1 percent of the world's children but 40 percent of its Little Tikes basketball hoops and other toys.
- Big warehouse stores have fueled unprecedented levels of stockpiling food and other items.

• Three out of four American garages are too full to hold cars.

Researchers also identified a trend among families that had acquired a large number of physical possessions: it elevated levels of stress hormones in the family but particularly for mothers. Science is finally catching up to what we, as spiritual beings, have always believed (even if we didn't always live it)—that simplicity and joy go hand in hand and that clutter and accumulation lead to stress and noise. While movements such as the KonMari method of cleaning made famous by Marie Kondo popularize our desire to live simple and more uncluttered lives, the heart of simplicity is not the things we keep or the things we give away. More deeply, it is how clutter affects us spiritually, which in turn affects us mentally, emotionally, and physically.

The Link between Simplicity and Stillness

The concept of intentional simplicity may seem like a new one, but it has been an interwoven part of the Celtic tradition for thousands of years and also part of the Christian tradition. Indeed, Jesus confronted the "rich young man" in the Gospels because of his love of possessions with the words "Go, sell what you possess and give to the poor." He asks the rich young man to "come, follow me." But we are told that "when the young man heard this statement, he went away sad, for he had many possessions" (Matthew 19:21–22). The rich young man was so attached to the possessions he loved that he walked away from the source of love itself: Jesus Christ. There are many rich young men and women today who walk away from relationships, love, joy, and peace all because they cling to their possessions. If we hold on to what we value, then we have to search our hearts and ask ourselves, what or whom do we truly value?

Is there a link between physical and spiritual clutter? Pope Francis certainly thinks so. At the canonization of Óscar Romero on October

18, 2018, Pope Francis reminded us that "the problem is on our part: our having too much, our wanting too much, suffocates our hearts and makes us incapable of loving." There is nothing wrong with surrounding ourselves with objects that bring us joy or have a story connected to them, unless we become too attached and distracted by them like the "rich young man" in the Bible. Decluttering our lives can free us to look more deeply at how we live and how we love. Decluttering helps us discard ways of being that do not strengthen us in faith. In his "First Principle and Foundation," St. Ignatius speaks of "making use of those things that help bring us closer to God and leaving aside those things that do not." If you are filling the hole in your heart with all kinds of possessions, know that it is a bottomless well you cannot feed.

A quote that has been attributed to many different sources sums it up as follows: "Things are made to be used and people are made to be loved but we love things and use people." We are moved, transformed, and experience growth through the wisdom of others. How we live affects how others live, and if we live with simplicity of heart, it will positively affect our relationships. It is often harder to say no to the constant drive toward materialism that pushes the narrative that we have to accumulate and consume more in order to be happy. It takes more intentionality to live a life of simplicity than excess. It is easier to give in to our pleasures and whims, living beyond our means until our homes become places that are cluttered and distracting, just as the world is. But it is worth it to say no. Saying no to stuff and to stress means saying yes to simplicity. And in living simply we find that we have more time for stillness and retreat.

Stillness Is Golden

Stillness and silence are related but not the same. We tend to think of silence as quietness or the absence of noise, but stillness is a much deeper "thin" practice. You can be silent but not at rest. Stillness is not just about the lack of noise but is the practice of sacred listening and rest on the level of soul. Stillness of heart and mind sets the stage for encounter with God. In the Psalms we are urged to "be still and know that I am God" (Psalm 46:10). When we are present (being) and still, it is then that we will have knowledge or wisdom of God. Stillness is a masterful teacher for it is in the dark spaces of our hearts that God speaks. The older I get, the more I appreciate the gift of stillness. If God is the creator of our souls, then the architect of the cathedral of our souls is stillness. Often in our conversations we are so busy listening to respond that we forget to be still and be present to what is spoken and what is unspoken. Many people today do not feel truly listened to. When we are not listened to, we are not understood. We feel that nobody really knows who we are or nobody cares enough to listen to us and so we become a prisoner of loneliness.

Our journey is a deep soul well of accumulated values and experiences from which we draw strength. Not all that we accumulate is necessary and good. As we go through life, we become aware of all that we have accumulated, the good and the bad, and we start the process of sifting through it. Some wells become stagnant over time and the water is not safe to drink. Other wells become cluttered with rubbish and trash. Working through the stillness of memory provides clarity and allows us to separate the helpful from the unhelpful.

The Irish *seanfhocal, Is maith an scéalaí an aimsir*, can be translated "time is a good storyteller," but there is another meaning here. Interestingly, the word *aimsir* means "weather" in Ireland, but it is also used in the sense of time and history. The double meaning here is that with time, of course, we can "weather" any storm, which is another way of saying that with the benefit of God's grace and a bit of time, we heal and we grow. Each of us ought to place a premium on stillness and, like St. Kevin of Glendalough, when the world becomes too rushed and noisy, seek out spaces for solitude similar to the mystics and the desert hermits of Egypt. The early Christian Celts were heavily influenced by the early desert hermits and Desert Fathers and Mothers of Egypt such as Anthony the Great, Sarah of the Desert, and John Cassian. Beginning around the third century, these early hermits lived mainly in the Scetis Desert of Egypt and greatly influenced the Celtic saints. The Irish word *ysert* or *diser*, meaning "desert," comes from the Latin word *disertum*. Today it retains its original meaning, referring to a place of solitude or a retreat for a more intimate encounter with God.

Even going to Mass, we often need reminders of the need for silence and stillness to aid in our contemplation and worship. There is a church in Graiguecullen in County Carlow that has a beautiful Celtic plaque on the outside door that reads

> Enter this door as if the floor within were gold,
> And every wall of jewels, all wealth untold:
> As if a choir in robes of fire were singing here.
> Nor shout,
> Nor rush,
> But hush,
> For God is here.

Never doubt the reality that "God is here." God is with you as you cry through your pain. God is with you as you smile though your heart is breaking. God is with you when your soul is flooded with joy. God is there in the midst of whatever you are going through right now. God is there in your joys and triumphs. God is here with you right now, in the space between the words on this page and the stirrings of your soul. God is here.

Your Thin Place: Creating a Space for Grace, Part II

Breaking Open

Irish seanfhocal (old word): An té a thabharfas
scéal chugat tabharfaidh sé dhá scéal uait.
Translation: Whoever will bring a story to
you, will take two stories from you.

This Irish phrase reminds us that when we share with others, whether it be a story or a meal, we often leave with far more in the goodness that has been extended to us.

Breaking Through

- How can you practice the art of radical hospitality?
- What are some areas of your life where you might adopt a *meitheal* mindset?
- Which areas of your life are more cluttered than you like?
- How might you cultivate time for stillness each day?
- Have you ever gone on a retreat? Would you consider going on one?

Breaking Free

Offer hospitality to one another
without grumbling.

—1 Peter: 4:9

- Invite your neighbors to your home for a meal.
- Notice who needs help and extend yourself generously.
- Give freely without expecting to receive.
- Reduce material and visual clutter in your life.
- Keep only those items or collections that bring you joy.

- Examine your relationship with your possessions. Pay attention to what has been hoarded, what is sparse, and what you have just enough of.
- Set aside a day to recharge: no devices, social media, internet, or screens.
- Send thank-you notes.

Epilogue: A Homecoming for Your Soul

Here's "the Thing."

For many years, I couldn't bring myself to look at the Thing. On the morning that I said goodbye to my mother for the last time, I went to pick up my family at the airport. As I mentioned before, my husband, Wayne, had driven four hours to Chicago with a three- and a nearly-one-year-old and then flown eight hours to Ireland, knowing that time was slipping away. All by himself.

I kissed my mother goodbye and told her I loved her and that I'd be home soon. Her breath was faint, but I could tell that she could hear me and she nodded in response. At the airport, the children were excited to be in Ireland, and my husband was exhausted—he was on his twenty-sixth hour without sleep. On the way back home, we stopped to refuel and get a snack. In the store, my eyes were drawn to some circular pottery hanging by a chain. Was it a round bird feeder? I wondered. Or a pretty red garden ornament? Not really sure what it was, I was drawn to the Celtic designs that were etched all around the circle, and so I bought it. With the shopping and snacks, we spent twenty minutes in the shop and left.

About twenty minutes from town, I received a call: Mam had died. Finding it too painful to look at, I hid the Thing away.

That's the Thing—regret, loss, pain, brokenness, addiction, shame, abuse—we never really know what someone is carrying on the inside. Life is often a series of those "darn things" that we don't know what to do with. That includes grief, loss, and regret. Sometimes we cope, and sometimes we stuff the Thing away. We don't always get to choose what thing takes our breath away or holds us back. It was only after eight years that I took out the Thing and hung it up. With time and patience, the Thing has been transformed. It is now a thin place for me. The Thing hasn't changed, but I have. With the eyes of the soul, I now see a red circle symbolizing the unending circle of love that unites us all. More personally for me, it symbolizes the love my mother and I shared; the hole in the center is the void that was left in my own heart when she died. That's the Thing. That's my thin place. What's the Thing for you?

My prayer is that each of us one day will hold the Thing that we most keep hidden, give thanks to God for what it teaches us, and set it free.

If life is a circle, beginnings and endings ebb and flow into one another, just as the Celts believed.

Years later, I went home to Ireland for Christmas and ran into Sister Anne at the local shop. It had been fifteen years since we had last seen each other. "Julianne, you haven't changed a bit," she said. "You still have that same mischievous sparkle in your eye." She laughed. I burst out laughing because I could have said the exact same thing about her!

But then she stopped, put her two hands on either side of my face, and looked deeply into my eyes. "Oh, but you have changed," she said with great emotion in her voice. "I see the suffering. I see the living." And with that, she wrapped me in a great big hug.

"Who are you?" Sister Anne had asked me at a time in my life when all I had were empty words. Many years have passed since I attempted to answer her question, and my soul journey has answered this question in its own way, just as yours does or will. While the world presents humanity as a jumble of biology, fragments of nerves and cells, neurological processes, and complex DNA, we are far more than an amalgam of physical properties. We are spiritual beings. But today in a world rich in everything but simplicity, silence, and truth, we are distracting ourselves into spiritual oblivion. Spirituality has become divorced from relationship with God as we fashion God in our own image: a hyperconnected God who we imagine favors the image of what is on the outside instead of what is on the inside. The push to be better, faster, richer, and more complex has left many of us choosing a different path for our lives: a simple path, in the journey of faith, well trodden before us and well trodden after us. A spiritual path. A path that opens us up to the thin spaces inside us and before us.

When I think of Gandhi's famous phrase "I like your Christ but not your Christians," I am reminded of the responsibility that comes with being a person of faith. While there are no perfect people, the broken road of faith is filled with potholes of hypocrisy, intolerance, and discrimination, some institutional and structural in nature, but mostly of our own making. St. Patrick presented Christianity in such a way that it met the needs of a deeply searching people, and today we must do the same. We must earn the right to be heard by loving others in such a way that they ask what the source of our joy, compassion, and sense of inner peace is. I believe that anyone who wants to love others completely and deeply is at heart a mystic. Mystics tap into "thin places" where the supernatural and the natural come together. *Mysticism* can mean many things but I believe that it is simply the direct experience of God. It is an abandonment to the adventure of living with "holy worldliness" as we try to experience in the thin places the wild things of God. Jesus Christ urged us to love with abandon with the words "Love one another. As I have loved you, so you must love one another" (John 13:34). We must love ourselves and others with complete abandon.

There are few certainties in life but two that define us: we will be born, and we will die. What we consider "to be born" may be a death and what we consider death and "the end" may be a new life. The soul's journey is a circle through life, death, and rebirth. There is no ending, for in our journey through life, death is one stop in a road that leads elsewhere, and there is a certainty for each of us in this.

Our journey through life is a pilgrimage of the soul coming home to itself. "The soul is the source of its own unfolding," declared Heraclitus, the first-century BC philosopher who lived in ancient Ephesus. The unfolding, I believe, is the journey of coming home to who we were created to be.

"Who are you?" Sister Anne asked me again.

My soul spoke for me: "I am God's child. I am enough. I am at peace—I have broken free."

About the Author

JULIANNE STANZ is a storyteller, encourager, and retreat leader who grew up in Ireland and now serves as Director of Parish Life and Evangelization for the Diocese of Green Bay. She is also a consultant to the Committee on Evangelization and Catechesis of the USCCB.

Acknowledgments

The writing process is always a sort of thin place where friends and pilgrims journey together, and this book is no different.

Father David McElroy, Opraem, thank you for your eloquence and your Irish wit and wisdom all dispensed over cups of tea. I am grateful that we are family.

Msgr. Jim Feely, soul friend and spiritual director; your presence in my life is a continual gift.

To Bishop David L. Ricken and Bishop David O'Connell: thank you for praying with me and for me and for encouraging me to keep writing.

To the students of the Milwaukee Irishfest Summer School, who for many years have attended my classes on Celtic Spirituality: our ten years together have been a blessing.

To the team at Loyola Press, especially Joellyn, Gary, Carrie, Joe, and Vinita: thank you for believing in this project. I could not have done it without you.

Also by Julianne Stanz

Start with Jesus
How Everyday Disciples Will
Renew the Church

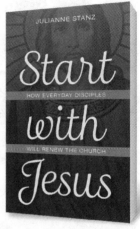

Serving parishes in her diocese as the
Director of New Evangelization, Author
Julianne Stanz has recognized a practical
and motivational way to restructure
a parish's mission—start with Jesus.
Start with Jesus is a book about people,
process, and culture, rather than an
emphasis on quick fixes or unsustainable
efforts. Julianne Stanz aims to help
regular people be transformed from the
inside out by growing in relationship with
Jesus Christ through individual and group
experiences, thus transforming our parish
communities.

Start with Jesus will be an essential
resource for decision-makers and
thought-leaders in parishes, but its true
strength lies in its value for the countless
Catholics longing for peace, healing,
and hope in the context of our parish
communities. It will be an inspiration to
Catholics who come to Mass each week,
parents trying to instill the faith in their
children, leaders searching for an effective
and sustainable approach to parish
renewal, and to all who are curious about
developing a relationship with Jesus.

PAPERBACK | 978-0-8294-4884-9 | $17.95

To Order:

Call 800.621.1008, visit store.loyolapress.com, or visit your local bookseller.

Also by Julianne Stanz

Developing Disciples of Christ

Developing Disciples of Christ explores a
Catholic understanding of evangelization
grounded in Scripture and Tradition, the
inseparable nature of content and methodology
in catechesis, and so much more.

ENGLISH: PAPERBACK | 978-0-8294-4528-2 | $13.95
SPANISH: PAPERBACK | 978-0-8294-4671-5 | $13.95

The Catechist's Backpack

The Catechist's Backpack fosters, explores,
and celebrates the spirituality of the catechist
and encourages catechists to embrace their
spirituality and pass on a living faith to those
they teach.

ENGLISH: PAPERBACK | 978-0-8294-4246-5 | $9.95
SPANISH: PAPERBACK | 978-0-8294-4421-6 | $9.95

To Order:

Call 800.621.1008, visit store.loyolapress.com, or visit your local bookseller.